Supporting Special Educational Needs in Secondary School Classrooms

M.

Second Edition

Supporting Special Educational Needs in Secondary School Classrooms

Second Edition

Jane Lovey

David Fulton Publishers
London

David Fulton Publishers Ltd
Ormond House, 26–27 Boswell Street, London WC1N 3JZ

www.fultonpublishers.co.uk

First published in Great Britain in 1995 by David Fulton Publishers

Second edition 2002

Note: The right of Jane Lovey to be identified as the author of this work has been asserted by her in accordance with the Copyright, Designs and Patents Act 1988.

British Library Cataloguing in Publication Data
A catalogue record for this book is available from the British Library.

ISBN 1–85346–832–0

Typeset by Elite Typesetting Techniques, Eastleigh, Hampshire
Printed in Great Britain by The Cromwell Press Ltd, Trowbridge, Wilts.

Contents

Acknowledgements

My heartfelt thanks go to all those working in the schools where I carried out the research that made it possible to write this book in the first place, and then revise it seven years later. I thank you all for welcoming me into your schools and giving your time and expertise to me so freely. My thanks go also to all the parents and children who shared their thoughts and feelings with me and helped me to understand how it felt to be in an inclusive classroom.

It is to all these people I dedicate the revised version of this book.

I also wish to thank my friend Valli Melchior, without whose help in the final stages the manuscript would not have been completed.

CHAPTER 1

Introduction

In the early 1990s the off-site unit for excluded pupils, which I had run for 12 years, was closed. The Warnock Report was a decade old and the ideal of all students with special needs being supported in their neighbourhood school was being implemented. I was redeployed as a support teacher for those with statements of special needs in the borough's secondary schools. Faced with the requirement to do research in order to finish an MA, I set out to identify indicators of effective support in secondary school classrooms (Lovey 1995).

Research

During the Summer of 2000 I obtained a small research grant from Cambridge to go back and see what, if anything, had changed in the intervening seven years. In the original research I had interviewed heads, Special Needs Co-ordinators (SENCOs), subject teachers, learning support teachers (LSTs), parents, and last but by no means least, children. In the new research I added a new cohort of interviewees, teaching assistants (TAs) (formerly known as learning support assistants).

I took as a starting point the 11 indicators of effective support that had emerged in 1993:

- the personal involvement of the senior management team with the delivery of support, and high status given to the post of SENCO;
- good communication between all those concerned with the statemented child;
- time allocation for liaison between all the child's teachers and the parents;

- recognition of the link between learning difficulties and behavioural difficulties, and the building of self-esteem;
- a positive personality and philosophy on the part of the support teacher;
- the appointment of a special needs co-ordinator for each faculty, or subject area;
- availability of specialist advice for special educational needs;
- INSET provision;
- the facility for withdrawal for a specific purpose, even when the general policy is for in-class support;
- availability of material resources for support;
- covert delivery of support to some secondary school pupils, depending on the pupil's temperament.

Second time round

The first impression, when visiting the schools after seven years, was the progress that had been made during the intervening years. Where in 1993 heads and SENCOs were often struggling with the language of integration, in 2000 they were speaking the language of inclusion. It was difficult to believe that these were the professionals who had doubts whether their schools would be able to cope with the learning needs of students with severe physical, sensory and learning difficulties. The head who expressed grave reservations spoke proudly of the diversity of need for which the school was now catering: 'each time we gear up for a student with a different disability we become more inclusive'.

Another school that had been reluctant to accept a student with severe visual impairment (VI) had since taken three further students with VI, had used the monies from these statements to employ a VI specialist teacher and was seeking to be allowed to have a VI unit. Already this school was providing informal outreach to other schools, including advice and practical help with preparing large print and Braille texts.

Parental choice

This advice was welcomed by schools which had no experience of visual impairment, which had nevertheless been named as the chosen school on a statement of special need for a child with VI. This was one of the underlying conflicts that existed alongside the tremendous progress that had been made in inclusion. It seemed to most to be common sense that students with a definite disability, such as VI, should be sent to a secondary school where there were people with experience and expertise in this disability. However, could that simply create another 'special school system' within mainstream? The borough that was researched is a small borough, seven miles across its widest point, with a good system of public transport, so that a student could reach any school within 30 minutes. An ideal situation, perhaps, to have some element of specialisation in some of the 14 secondary schools.

Two students with visual impairment were due to transfer to secondary school during the following September. One boy already had two brothers at the only boys' school, that his father and uncles had also attended. The family was determined that he should also attend this school. The other, a girl with a degenerative disease, had from an early age set her heart on going to the convent school where all the females in her family had been educated for many years. Thus, although there existed a mixed comprehensive with experience and expertise in VI, two other schools were in receipt of informal outreach support. This was the reasoning behind the borough holding back on establishing a dedicated unit in one school for VI.

When these cases were followed up in December, at the end of their first term at their secondary school, SENCOs who had previously had misgivings, spoke enthusiastically of the personalities of both students. They had certainly brought challenges, but the schools had risen to those challenges and were now convinced that the parents were right in putting their child's feelings before their disability. So often it seemed that professionals, who were overwhelmed by the case papers of a student, were completely won over by the individual personality.

There was one case in which parental choice did not best serve the needs of their children. In 1997 a new secondary school had been built in the borough and was oversubscribed from the beginning. The parents of two children with dyslexia and dyspraxia had named this school on the statement of their first son, and the following year had chosen this school for their second son also. Both boys had to catch two buses as they travelled from the opposite side of the borough to this school. Because of the nature of their disability they were often late. Sometimes they left PE kit or other equipment on one of the buses or at the bus stop where they transferred from one bus to the other. The situation was made more absurd by the fact that they changed buses outside a school where the SENCO and a number of well-established staff are known to have expertise in dyslexia and dyspraxia.

The head teacher of the latter school had warned the parents that the new school had a SENCO who was 'learning on the job' and they could not claim any expertise in this area. During the first year that this school had opened it had been named on 12 statements despite having no track record for special needs. One of these statements concerned a girl with mobility problems and her choice was totally valid since it had been built with lifts for students in wheelchairs, and with other mobility aids. The facilities at this school will be described in some detail in Chapter 8.

Emotional and behavioural difficulties

All schools had tremendous concerns about students with emotional and behavioural difficulties. This was the one group of students for whom it was sometimes difficult to see the advantages of being in a mainstream school. This will be discussed in detail in Chapters 6 and 7. Of the students who were interviewed two were more troubled than troublesome, however, the heads and teachers spoke mainly about those who were troublesome and presented constant, and sometimes intolerable, challenges in the classroom.

One young teacher commented that 'exclusion is instead of special schools now, isn't it?', and her two companions nodded sagely. In fact there were students who were often temporarily excluded, excluded until parents came to speak to the head of year, excluded from certain lessons, set work to do in the corridor, or outside the head's office. When they were in class it was often with a TA placed between them and the other children. When asked how she would cope with a very disruptive student, one head immediately said, 'Oh, she would have to have one-to-one. Yes, she would have to have a minder with her all the time.' There were students who were under close surveillance all the time they were in classrooms. Perhaps the question has to be asked whether this really is inclusion.

Indicators of effective support

SENCO status
Apparently some of the heads had received a list of these indicators after the 1993 research was completed, and had worked towards achieving them. The enhanced status of the SENCO and his or her increased involvement with the Senior Management Team (SMT) was very much in evidence. Without exception SENCOs had much more time to do their job. During the time of the first research they were looking forward to the Code of Practice and wondering what difference it would make to their workload. During the revisiting of the research it was clear that the Code had placed tremendous

burdens on the shoulders of stressed SENCOs during the first few years. However, heads and boards of governors had recognised that without allowing the resources they could not expect the statutory work to be done. Consequently there were no longer Maths or English teachers who were SENCOs on the side, but SENCOs had status for their special needs role.

In 1993 many of the SENCO were volunteers, or teachers who were 'good with the weaker ones', and had been asked to take on the job. In 2000 some of these professionals had become very skilled and confident in their posts. There were others who had 'cut their teeth' elsewhere and were on their second or third post as a SENCO. These teachers brought expertise from other situations. Many of the SENCOs had done diplomas and MAs in Special Needs, and were confidently running departments with six or more TAs and occasionally one or two LSTs. In most cases the line manager was the deputy head, and they met regularly with the SMT.

Communication
This remained a problem area, not because of a lack of will to communicate but a lack of time. Liaison with parents depended totally on the goodwill of staff who used time before school, lunch-times and after school to see parents, since most non-contact time was used for statutory statement reviews (where SENCOs hoped parents would attend!).

Whereas nine years ago teachers had supported students with special needs in secondary school classrooms (LSTs), there are now teaching assistants. Concerns about TAs will be dealt with in Chapter 2. However this is an area where the lack of dedicated time to liaise can cause great difficulties. Such LSTs who were still employed also felt a need of more time to maximise the contribution they could make, although because most had been around for six or seven years they had learned to grab quick consultations with teachers in the staff rooms.

Individual Educational Plans had redeemed what could have been an impossible situation. However, these had to be well written, not too ambitious, and distributed to all staff (and read by them) who taught the student. In one school these were reviewed termly by the form teacher, who moved up through the school with the student. This seemed to provide excellent opportunity for real communication, since the form teacher also had facility to liaise with parents.

Link between learning difficulties, behavioural difficulties and self-esteem.
The teachers and support staff recognised the clear links between these three elements and worked hard to raise the self-esteem of the students they were supporting. Many spoke of trying to 'catch them being good' (CBG)

(Montgomery 1989) before students started to show frustration with their learning, in outbursts of bad behaviour.

In interviews with parents it became apparent that many of those who had a statement listing both learning and behaviour difficulties had suffered learning difficulties from an early age at primary school but had only developed behavioural difficulties at the end of the primary phase, or on transfer to secondary.

Silly and disruptive behaviour was often used to put up a smokescreen around a student who would otherwise be exposed as having learning difficulties. One boy said: 'I am my own worst enemy. I like to be the class clown because I know I can't do the work. Then I go too far and I end up shouting at the teacher, and then running out.' This boy was dyslexic and dyspraxic. His mother belonged to the national organisations and had explained all his difficulties to the secondary school before he went there. His main difficulty was being unable to copy from the white or chalk board while sitting in his seat. At the beginning teachers gave him what had to be written on a piece of paper to have on his desk, but they did not do this for the homework. At home he either did not have the homework written down or he could not read what he had written. He was then reprimanded for not having done his homework. This would provoke an 'incident'. This problem and the problems of other students with these difficulties will be dealt with in Chapter 5.

Self-esteem is such an important factor in this study that Chapter 3 will be devoted to this. All schools were consciously addressing the issue of boosting the self-esteem of students with special educational needs.

The personality of the support teacher or assistant, and the compatibility between members of classroom teams
When Fergusson and Adams (1983), Best (1991) and Thomas (1992) wrote about classroom teams this was a fairly novel concept. Since then teachers have become accustomed to leading a classroom team. Indeed newly trained teachers have known nothing else. With the advent of TAs there can often be more than one support worker in the classroom and any tension or unease between adults in the classroom is likely to hinder the learning and affect the behaviour of the adolescents.

Nurture Groups and early intervention for little children are based largely on the relationship between the team of two (a teacher and a learning assistant) who run the group (Bennathan and Boxall 2000). Secondary school students often benefit from similar 'nurturing' on their arrival at secondary school. This is especially the case if they know they have difficulties with learning.

Personality and philosophy

In the first research project these aspects emerged as being extremely important. The concept of having a second adult in a classroom was quite a new one for most secondary teachers, and at that time the second adult was usually a qualified teacher. There were two issues here. Firstly the class teacher sometimes felt very exposed, especially if the support teacher was a retired head teacher or someone redeployed from a defunct special school. Secondly the support teacher had usually been accustomed to managing a class, and in some cases a department or a school. Now they were sitting next to individual children in the classroom during much of the lesson. It took time for classroom culture to change to the extent that the second adult felt free to move around while the 'lead' teacher was delivering the substance of the lesson. There were also potential tensions when adolescents inevitably tested the boundaries. It was important that the support teacher was able to sit calmly in the class room and read unspoken signals from the 'lead' teacher. Both teachers needed to have a will to make working together effective for the children, even if sometimes it meant hiding feelings and deferring to each other.

There were horror stories of support teachers who had stood up in the classroom and inappropriately berated the class for behaviour that was acceptable to the teacher, just as support teachers related how the teacher had turned from the board and demanded to know who was talking. Often it was the support teacher explaining the work to a student with special needs. These incidents became fewer and fewer, and when they did happen were often treated with humour. However, not every teacher has the philosophy and personality to be able to make some of the compromises necessary.

This was an area that had changed a great deal since, in the intervening years, a second adult in the classroom became the norm rather than an exception. One of the main differences is that now the second adult is more often than not a learning support assistant. The following chapter will chart the change from support teachers to support assistants. The advantage of the latter, apart from cost, is that they come into the classroom without having to shed their previous lead role. They have also started to work in classrooms at a time when teachers are used to having a second adult and are much more used to utilising regular support in the classroom.

Nevertheless, the philosophy and personality is still important. One teacher spoke of a TA who was: 'very quiet and always seems quite grim. I always feel that she disapproves of me although she says nothing. She only speaks when spoken to and I always feel I have to chose my words very carefully.'

I am not sure how important compatibility is in the current situation where a TA is often receiving training and is in a learning situation. However, if the two adults have very different expectations of students' behaviour there can be tensions. Compatibility is more important where both are teachers, as one inevitably is the leader and it is important that the one in the other position is comfortable with the situation.

SEN link teachers

In 1993 only two schools had a co-ordinator in each subject who had sight of all the statements of special need and took responsibility for organising support within the department. This is now almost the norm, although in some schools it is only done in Maths, English and Science. One of the current SENCOs had developed her interest in special needs through being the Maths link teacher in her school, and a Science link teacher was looking for a post as a SENCO.

A very important role of the link teacher is to keep track of resources for students, keep up to date with equipment that is constantly becoming available through specialist manufacturers, and make sure the equipment is available throughout the department. It is also important that the teacher of the student with special needs can discuss with the link teacher what impact the needs have on how the child learns, and how work in that subject might be affected.

Availability of specialist advice and INSET provision

This is placed after the previous section because this is the order in which the issues appeared after a factor analysis of the interviews in the 1993 research. This would now be much further up the agenda, since other issues have been resolved and schools are confidently accepting students with more complex difficulties. In each school the SENCO or an individual teacher related an account of training that had taken place as the direct result of a specific child coming into the school. In one case this was a boy with Asperger syndrome. The SENCO went on a one-day course on this. As well as sharing what she had learnt with staff on the INSET day before the boy was due to start, she had invited a speaker from the local Asperger's group. This woman had been a teacher as well as the mother of a grown-up son with Asperger syndrome. Staff said how useful this day had been. It had given them confidence and made them much more understanding of the boy. (More information about coping with students with Asperger syndrome and autism is given in Chapters 6 and 7.)

Pressure groups, often started by parents, and chaired by other experts, are an excellent source of information, and can often provide good INSET presenters. Details of helpful organisations are provided in the Appendix.

Another useful source of information is the Internet, if used with caution. Most of the support groups have their own sites, and they are normally fairly reliable. Many of the sites are American. While being very interesting, and sometimes based on research, the context is often quite different from British schools.

Withdrawal

The philosophy towards withdrawal has changed a great deal in the borough in which the research was done. In 1993 there were schools that took single, or small groups of students, out of the classroom for specific programmes but they were apologetic about this. On the whole the rule was no withdrawal under any circumstance. Structured programmes to teach dyslexic students strategies for spelling were often undertaken in the corner of a busy classroom during registration/form time, or during lunch-times and at the end of the day.

Parents were crying out for their offspring to have some help away from the classroom, and thought that this is what one-to-one meant on a statement. However, this was only rarely allowed.

In 2000, such support 'teachers', rather than assistants, as were still employed by the schools often spent a significant proportion of their time with groups of students doing specific structured literacy programmes. In most of the schools where this happened it took the place of a second foreign language. No parent had complained about the second language being missed for this. It did, however, mean that the child selected for a literacy programme in Year 8 would not be able to subsequently return to German if the structured programme was sufficient to solve the literacy problem. It appeared that there were only two students, in two different schools, who improved to the level where they really no longer needed withdrawal. Since six schools had between 12 and 20 students on these programmes this was not seen to be a real problem.

The literacy programmes were planned for Years 8 and 9. In Years 10 and 11 these were known as support groups and, in theory, students were to bring with them course work they needed to catch up on. In practice this was a problem as students often arrived with no work and could not be allowed to disturb the class where their work was in order to fetch it. It was known that they all had work with which they needed help. It appeared that after years of struggling at school many of those for whom support was provided had already given up battling.

Material resources

Although all the schools were struggling to withstand constant cuts in budgets, there were reasonable resources available. Nine years previously printing out work done on a laptop was often difficult but is now an accepted procedure for a number of students. Children who needed them usually had received laptops. However, there was an ongoing problem with machines that went wrong and took weeks to repair.

In one school the head had used the proceeds of the summer fête to supplement the special needs budget so that textbooks with a suitable level of literacy for the lowest streams could be purchased. The provision of resources was still patchy, and often dependent upon the SENCO's persistence with a begging bowl. Often quite important pieces of equipment and software had been obtained by local fund-raising and collecting supermarket vouchers.

Covert delivery of support

This is the last issue on the 1993 list of indicators but, in interviews based on the 12 indicators, teachers often selected this issue as being very important. The child who will accept the help of an adult in Year 7, by Year 8 often appeared to prefer to be reprimanded for bad behaviour than admit that he, or occasionally she, needed help. TAs expressed their frustration at being allocated to support a student who was aggressive to them at every approach and refused any offer of help.

One 15-year-old girl interviewed desperately wanted the help but did not want her friends to know she needed it. She admitted that she always told the TA to go away, and then tried to hear what she was saying to others. She admitted that she often shouted at the teacher for not teaching properly, rather than accept help!

It is very difficult to support these students unless there is a student nearby with a similar difficulty to whom the work can be explained in a stage whisper. If one is aware of specific difficulties that might occur, perhaps a tape could be made to explain a process in stages to the student, or a set of diagrams if it is a Science or Technology lesson. If difficulties occur with spelling, perhaps a discreet one-to-one session, making sure the student has a dictionary, and knows how to use it, would be helpful. It is important that if there is a statement recommending classroom support, and the student is rejecting it, that the SENCO is aware of this.

Conclusion

In 1993 there was a feeling sometimes of picking one's way through uncharted territory. Seven years later, not only was the language of inclusion being spoken unselfconsciously by most of the professionals interviewed, but inclusion was happening. Heads who had said that integration would not work were proud of the inclusiveness of their schools. The only real problem was including students with the 'acting out' types of emotional and behavioural difficulties. This will be dealt with in two separate chapters.

In the first edition of this book the second chapter, 'Always a Bridesmaid, Never a Bride' was about the role of the learning support teachers at that time. In this edition the next chapter will mainly examine the role of the TA and will look again at the changed role of support teachers, where they have survived in an ever tougher market-place.

Further reading

Cheminais, R. (2001) *Special Educational Needs for Newly Qualified and Student Teachers: A Practical Guide*. London: David Fulton Publishers.

Garner, P. and Davies, J. D. (2001) *Introducing Special Educational Needs: Guide for Students*. London: David Fulton Publishers.

Thomas, G., Walker, D. and Webb, J. (1998) *The Making of the Inclusive School*. London: Routledge.

CHAPTER 2

Supporting Roles

In the first edition of this book, this chapter was about teachers who had suddenly found themselves in a supporting role in the classroom. Many of the teachers had been staff at special schools and were taking part in the process to integrate their pupils into mainstream schools. In many cases the staff of the school had become an outreach service, working with their previous pupils and their mainstream teachers in their classrooms (Bannister, C. *et al.* 1998). This was a very positive role since initially pupils benefited greatly from being supported by familiar adults, and the adults had a well-defined role.

Other support teachers had been redeployed from centrally funded services which were disbanding. This disbanding was often a direct result of schools leaving the LEA to become Grant Maintained, and taking funds for special needs out of the budget. Some authorities delegated special needs monies to schools to prevent them leaving the system. This meant that an number of teachers who had worked outside schools, often in advisory or specialist roles, found themselves supporting in other teachers' classrooms. Although many teachers adapted well to this role, there were some tensions. In secondary schools, at the beginning of the 1990s, teachers were not used to having a colleague, except a technician, working alongside them, and could feel threatened by a perceived 'expert' in the classroom.

The other source of support in the classroom were subject teachers who had slots in their timetable filled with support periods in the classrooms of colleagues. Often they were timetabled to go into a class where they had no experience of the subject.

Support dilemmas

There were a number of concerns about how support teachers should work. These were documented by Best (1991) and Thomas (1992a,b). Thomas (1999) lists some of the concerns which are still not resolved:

- Should TAs and/or support teachers only concentrate on the designated child or should they work with the rest of the class, as available and as necessary?
- Should children be withdrawn from the classroom for special work?
- Should all support be provided in the classroom?
- Should there be a combination of withdrawal and support?
- Who is the TA supporting – the child or the class teacher?
- What sort of training do TAs need?
- How can staff from non-education agencies be included fully in the support process at school?

The questions I asked heads, subject teachers, support staff and SENCOs during my research sought answers to these dilemmas. However, as explained in the last chapter, despite progress having been made in most areas the necessary time for forward planning is still not available. Until classroom teams (Thomas 1992a,b) can sit down and plan for the children, classroom support is unlikely to reach its full potential. It is difficult to answer these questions given this major constraint.

Progress

Just as there was a change in teachers' use of the language of inclusion, there was an increased ease with which they worked with others in the classroom. Whereas in 1993 most support in the classroom was given by qualified teachers, in 2000 it was mainly provided by an army of TAs. It is possible that some of the teachers, who were defensive and felt threatened when supported by another teacher, were more sure of the classroom roles when the other person was clearly an assistant.

Because TAs had largely replaced learning support teachers (LSTs), there were more of them in the classroom. As one head said: 'TAs are great. I am appointing four more next week. I can have four for the price of one teacher.' (!) One has to ask whether the quality of support given by a TA is 'good enough' and whether the employment of a second qualified teacher is wasteful of that person's skills (Margerison 1997).

The role of the LST

Two of the learning support teachers interviewed expressed a degree of frustration that new staff saw them as TAs and were unwilling to give them any responsibility on trips out, or during events at school such as comic-relief days. However, in all the secondary schools in the project, the LSTs did have a distinct role in that they took groups of dyslexic (Specific Learning Difficulties) children out of the classroom for specialised help. In some cases these students were permanently withdrawn from their second modern language, in others they were withdrawn from different subjects on a rotational basis.

Three of the LSTs also did a considerable amount of special needs administration and were right-hand assistants to their overburdened SENCOs. They often drew up and reviewed IEPs and prepared the reports for statement reviews. It was clear that the three teachers who had taken part in the research seven years ago now had tremendous expertise in a number of very specific special needs. All had experience of supporting students with Asperger syndrome through their secondary education.

In two schools the LSTs spoke of teachers who liked to feel in control of the learning of the students with special needs. Therefore, they would work on a regular basis with the special needs students on their course work, and the support teacher would lead the rest of the class. This reflects the 'room management' strategy, written about by Thomas *et al.* (1999). In these schools the LSTs were extremely well established.

More recently appointed LSTs had often agreed to work for a negotiated salary since they recognised that they did not have such a great after-school commitment. Those who were employed as teachers sometimes felt they were resented by their hard-pressed colleagues, because they did not have the same workload in terms of marking and lesson preparation. For this reason they often felt embarrassed about asking teachers to spare time to discuss forthcoming lessons with them.

There were some teachers who were working as TAs and resented the fact that they were paid the unqualified rate. They had accepted the post as it fitted in with bringing up young families, but there was confusion about their role since they welcomed the chance to 'act as teachers', in doing withdrawal work and sharing a class. However, because of the status of their post, teachers were unsure to what extent they could give them these responsibilities.

Although some of the SENCOs did support in the classroom, since the advent of TAs other teachers did not have support periods written into their timetables. Some regretted this as they felt that they were developing an interest in special needs, and these sessions also offered them the rare opportunity to work beside a colleague.

The role of teaching assistants

The Code of Practice (DfE 1994) resulted in schools being obliged to provide one-to-one (1:1) provision for a number of children with special educational needs.

> The chief beneficiary of this individual model has been the learning support assistant (TA) with increased employment prospects, who is hired as the only economically viable means of helping children to reach their individual targets, or of using funding that is attached to an individual child... it is not fashionable to decry the work of TAs... while maintaining our admiration for [their] skills and qualities, we need to look hard at the outcome of TA support in schools... studies of schools, reputed to have good practice in SEN and inclusion, and found all too often the TA was the child's main teacher, doing all the planning, with little opportunity to liaise with the class teacher... cases where the teacher more or less ignored the child. (Gross 2000)

Gross goes on to say that often TAs have no training and yet their presence can alleviate the teacher of the burden of adapting the curriculum for a child with special needs. There was evidence of this in an independent school that had a sincere policy of integration, which was realised by giving a place in each class to a child with Down's syndrome or a hearing impairment. Each child with special needs had his or her own TA in the classroom. In some cases the child was following a totally different programme from the rest of the class.

For a number of reasons TAs are good news, and many of them are contributing greatly to the success of all the children in some lessons. One young teacher, to whom I spoke, said: 'there is a completely different atmosphere when a TA is in the lesson. I feel more relaxed and the students seem to feel that too.' It is noticeable that teachers who trained in the 1990s are used to having a second person in the classroom and adopt a very positive view towards the presence of an assistant.

Classroom management

If TAs are to work effectively they must be managed well (Jarwood 1999) and their role must be clear. In secondary schools this happens best when they are attached to a subject or faculty. Whether this happens is dependent on timetabling, personalities and whether TAs are attached to individual students. In two schools this had been the intention of the SENCO, but in both cases one or two of the TAs, objected to this since they were bored by always attending lessons in the same subject. There appeared to have been no debate before abandoning what seemed to work for others. In the study of TAs working in faculties described by Jarwood, TAs were asked to keep a record of when they felt 'involved in lessons', and when they felt 'isolated'. They were all happier in their work when they had discussions with the head of faculty, and a job description. They felt they were part of the team, and attended INSET with these teams.

Sometimes TAs were attached to Year groups and would go up through the school with that group. These TAs were managed by the SENCO, not the head of year. The management of TAs in secondary schools is very much the task of the SENCO, which means that there is often little effective management within the classroom unless the class teacher is motivated to take time to do this.

The TA is certainly most effective where the teacher possesses good management skills. This was particularly evident where the teacher managed to make time for regular meetings with TAs and gave them a scheme of work for the term or the half term, with the expectation that they would do some preparation for the lessons. Where the student to be supported had a visual, hearing or motor difficulty a specialist from outside the school might well perform some aspects of the management role.

In some schools teachers complained that they did not know whether the TA would be in the lesson or not. In one school a teacher referred to a TA by name and remarked: 'I never have any idea whether she will arrive or not. Sometimes I am several minutes into the lesson when she arrives. I would have done different work if I had known she was coming.' In an interview with the TA she expressed concern that in addition to her assistant teacher role she was the qualified first-aider for the school and therefore sometimes called away at the last moment and could not keep her commitments in class. Often frustrations were caused by the lack of systems of communication in large schools. Sometimes a child with special needs had been asked to give a message, and had either forgotten to do so or had not been understood by the teacher.

Even where TAs were regularly in lessons, they often felt stress since they were expected to be ready to 'help out' but did not always know when and where. There were always students ready to ask for help, but one could be encouraging dependency. Where there was insufficient management, TAs were often making decisions which had important financial implications.

For example, one TA interviewed spoke about the boy she had been appointed to support:

> 'William has emotional and behavioural difficulties. He is supposed to be quite bright, but he doesn't want to know. When I try to help him, he turns his back on me. He gets into trouble for not doing his work... he loses his temper. He has been excluded twice. I can't take to him so I have given up trying... There is this other boy, Clint, he has difficulty with spelling and keeping his work neat. I have taken a real shine to him and help him most of the time. He comes and sits near me. I even help him with his homework.'

When one thinks of the expense of meetings of well-paid professionals that lead to a decision that a student should have support in the classroom, it is a cause for concern that an untrained assistant can decide which boy receives the support. There are a number of training issues here since the delivery of support to students with emotional and behavioural difficulties (EBD) requires extremely careful planning, and support for the person who is providing it. One also has to ask whether the second boy mentioned above is learning to be over-dependent on an adult.

This is a further example of the fact that if TAs are to be effective, teachers must increase their management skills so that the TA's work has a focus and is matched to the learning style and personality of the student with the statement of special needs.

Who are the TAs?

When TAs were interviewed they were first asked how they had become teaching assistants. There were a number of routes into the classroom, but by far the most common was that of women who started being voluntary helpers in their children's schools. When a child was given one-to-one provision on a statement, the mother would be invited to undertake the support. Sometimes the TA had come up to the secondary school with the child she had supported in primary school. This was particularly the case with children with physical or medical needs. In other cases the mother had decided to go into secondary school when her own children did so, although not usually to the same secondary school.

Secondary schools were much more likely to advertise posts, and, of course, people with experience were more likely to be appointed. Experience varied at this stage. Sometimes when a support post became available someone in the school office would ask to be considered, since they knew both the school and the student. In one case a midday supervisor was asked if she would like to be the full-time TA for a totally blind girl with learning difficulties. In other schools lunch-time and playground supervisory staff were always offered any support work that was available.

There were qualified teachers and other graduates who applied for TA posts because they wished to return to the workplace part time, but wished to fulfil their family commitments during school holidays. There were also nursery nurses, one of whom had followed a child from nursery, through primary, to secondary. Others had worked at special schools that had been closed and were using their expertise in special needs in this capacity. There were also those who had been known by other staff at the school and whose names had been put forward when a support was needed for a new statement.

I met very few men support assistants. This is probably because of the low rate of pay and the lack of a career structure. The two I met were both leaving at the end of term, one to go into teacher training and the other to drive a bus. The one who was going into teacher training was doing support as a gap year activity, suggested by his mother who was a teacher. He said that one of his friends had done the same thing but had now decided not to teach!

Most TAs thoroughly enjoyed their work and said that they would not want to do anything else. They all felt that, compared to teachers, they were very low paid and saw little difference between their work and the work of teachers. All said that they would welcome training and a career structure.

However, although the borough in which they worked offered training courses for both primary and secondary TAs, some had not found the time to go on a course. They were reluctant to go on a course that lacked accreditation. Those who had been on the local authority courses had enjoyed them and said it had helped them to understand how children learnt. Two had decided to do the Open University courses in support. One was funding herself, but the school was funding the other one.

In a survey of TAs in secondary schools, conducted during a training course, in one authority during the period 1996–7, it was found that 80 per cent had no period of induction into the job (Dew-Hughes, D. *et al.* 1998). However, 33 per cent had observed some lessons before starting to work and 35 per cent had a named mentor. Among 264 TAs there were ten with an NNEB qualification and most were educated to O-level (GCSE) or above. However there were 22 with no qualifications. A desire for training in coping with students with emotional and behavioural difficulties was expressed by 76 per cent of the TAs. As in the two studies which form the basis for this book, for most TAs the fact that no paid time was allowed for liaising with teachers was a big problem.

Training needs of teaching assistants

> Many more schools have… chosen to appoint assistants to their staff in many cases instead of teachers, as a cost saving ploy. There are, of course, moral and professional implications in these decisions, particularly where the most vulnerable children in the system are seen to be entrusted to those members of staff who, on the face of it, are the least qualified to work with them. (Balshaw 1999)

In her book *Help in the Classroom*, Balshaw lists six principles of working with learning support assistants in the classroom:

- Roles and responsibilities: learning support assistants should be clear about their roles and responsibilities and not be 'piggies in the middle'.
- Communication: learning support assistants should be included in and understand the communication system in the school and not be left in 'no man's land'.
- Consistency in approach: TAs should be seen positively as part of the provision to meet children's and students' educational needs, not as 'dogsbodies'.
- A working team: TAs should be valued as members of a working team, not seen as the 'spy in the classroom'.
- Personal and professional skills: TAs should be encouraged to make use of their personal and professional skills, not treated as an 'overgrown pupil'.
- Staff development needs: TAs should be supported in the development of their professional skills, not left 'up in the air'.

Perhaps one of the problems with recognising the training needs of TAs is that we have all had experience of schools. No one would expect to work as a dental assistant without having time spent on them, teaching them specific tasks and skills. However, one study found that 80 per cent of TAs were expected to know just what to do.

In the study by Dew-Hughes *et al.* (1998), the majority of TAs were in the 40 to 50 age group, and the next highest group was those aged 30 to 40. The organisation of schools and the roles of personnel in schools have moved on since they were at school. Awareness of the roles and responsibilities of everyone in a school is essential for good communication. For this reason, part of the compulsory training for a TA in any school should be a carefully planned induction, where channels of communication are carefully and clearly defined.

In some cases it might be necessary to give some pointers to the privileged position one has when working in a classroom, and the duty of confidence which prohibits discussing the teacher with colleagues, or the children with other parents. TAs are often privy to papers on students which might have sensitive details of social and medical problems.

Few other paraprofessionals would work with people without having a supervisor or mentor to whom to refer professional matters and from whom to derive support. Part of the training for the job should be coordinated by the mentor who should be able to create relevant learning situations within the school. If the training of TAs is to have a successful output in terms of children's education, it is important that running alongside this is training for teachers in managing the TAs. There is little point in having well-trained assistants if they are going to be used as 'dogsbodies' or allowed to be in the classroom just waiting for the odd chance to be useful.

Training

Even now that initial teacher training is so school based, students are taught the rudiments of human development – physical, cognitive and emotional. TAs who had undergone courses that included child development had found this very useful.

Because TAs bring with them such varying life and work histories, it is fitting that there exist so many different types of training course. Most authorities run their own training course, but unless they have an arrangement with a college of Further or Higher Education these tend not to be award-bearing. However, they do give an insight into what is happening in the classroom in terms of learning styles, physical, social and emotional development and the curriculum.

Many TAs interviewed were attending courses at the local FE college and were working towards NVQs. These courses are the beginning of providing a career structure for TAs, who are currently paid on a low scale. At present there is no set formula for paying TAs, or for recognising their experience and expertise.

Specialist training

Some TAs had been on specialist courses on such subjects as Specific Learning Difficulties (Spld/dyslexia). This is a popular course since so many pupils and students with the recommendation of 1:1 support on their statements have this difficulty. A few TAs had been on courses provided by the British Dyslexia Association or the Staines Institute, and were thus qualified to use their training outside school also. This was usually an initiative taken at the TA's own expense but such courses often require a level of qualifications at entry, such as 4 or 5 GCSEs at levels A-C.

Students with hearing impairment are in need of good 'communicators' rather than ordinary TAs. This will entail initial training by the Hearing Impaired Service of the local authority. The work of maintaining expensive audio aids is now often handed over to communicators, releasing the expert teachers of the deaf to work in a wide range of schools in a single area, even though they might be based in one centre. For some deaf students the communicator must be able to interpret sign language in the classroom. The course for proficiency in British Sign Language (BSL) is in three parts, with certification at the end of each. The entry requirement is four GCSEs at the level A-C. For some TAs there might be a necessity to obtain further GCSEs in order to become well qualified. This will eventually have implications for any pay/career structure that emerges for TAs.

There are already many TAs who have a very important qualification: that of the NNEB (Nursery Nursing Enrolment Board). These TAs have had a rigorous and well-established training that has qualified them to work in a caring and nurturing role in early years classes and in special schools. It is the nursery nurse rather than the class teacher who is qualified to perform such procedures as administering rectal valium (in cases of epileptic seizures) or the anaphylactic pen (in cases of extreme allergic reaction). However, in many secondary schools these paraprofessionals are paid on the same scale as totally unqualified TAs.

Moving on

There are a number of TAs who decide that they would like to become teachers. Their time working in classrooms will certainly be an asset when applying for training. However, they will still have to have the minimum qualifications required for such a course.

Caveats

It is a cause for concern that inappropriate responsibilities are being thrust upon some TAs in secondary schools. In some schools it is the TA who implements the Personal Support Plan (PSP) when a child is excluded from the classroom for up to three weeks because of unacceptable behaviour. The onus is on the TA to obtain suitable work for that child from the teacher and to teach it. In the case of a Year 10 or 11 child, a number of new concepts could be taught during this time. The rest of the class are receiving their teaching from a well-qualified specialist in the subject as they prepare for their examinations. Is the student who is already having difficulties assumed to have equal access to the National Curriculum when his education is placed into the hands of an unqualified person?

There are also cases where TAs are claiming to be responsible for the Individual Educational Plans (IEPs) and chairing the statement reviews in a school. These are tasks which have been seen to need the expertise of the SENCO, who since 1994 has received increased training in these processes. Whereas it makes sense for the LST to relieve the SENCO of some of these duties, if they are delegated to an unqualified person surely special educational needs within a school will lose some of the status they have gained within the last decade.

Conclusion

Teaching assistants are certainly good news for those who have to balance the budget in a school. Most of them are conscientious, eager to improve the school life of the students they support, and claim to be extremely happy in their posts. They are not happy about their level of pay, and are unanimously eager for a career structure. Among comments heard were: 'we do as much as the teachers', 'our head said he would rather have one of us take the class than a poor supply teacher'. Although these comments might be true in some cases, the fact remains that TAs should be supervised in what they do. They should not be exploited by being asked to supervise whole classes when teaching staff are absent, nor should they be in a position to make decisions on provision for the individual special needs of students.

In many schools the statements on one or two students with special needs are seen as paying for the support of four or five students in class. A girl with an autistic spectrum difficulty, whose statement had recommended full time 1:1 support said:

> 'I should have support but it is quite difficult for me. Because I need help I am in a group with two people who can't read and two boys who are just bad. The support teacher has her hands full with them. I am supposed to ask her if I am not sure what the teacher meant about

anything but I cannot get her attention without making myself embarrassed.'

There were other similar situations where the student(s) whose statement(s) had provided the money for the TA were not receiving the quality or type of support needed but the letter of the law was being kept. This was not the fault of the subject teacher, or even the SENCO, but of those who make the decision about budgets.

Parents of statemented children also expressed concerns about the use of TAs. As one mother of a highly disruptive boy with specific learning difficulties said:

> 'We sweat blood to get him statemented and he was doing great at the dyslexic unit, but since he has been at secondary often he hasn't even had a real teacher. He spends a lot of his time outside the classroom with June and she was a dinner lady at his primary school. He needs more teaching than the others, not less.'

Unfortunately, if the recommendations for 1:1 support on statements are to be honoured, it is necessary to employ staff who are cheaper than trained teachers. It is therefore important to make sure they are well supervised, that they are successfully managed by teachers with expertise in special needs. All students must be taught by the subject teachers on regular occasions.

Further reading

Balshaw, M. H. (2000) *Help in the Classroom*, 2nd edn. London: David Fulton Publishers.

Fox, G. (2001) *Supporting Children with Behaviour Difficulties: A Guide for Assistants in Schools*. London: David Fulton Publishers.

Kent, F. (2001) 'All in a day's work', *Special!* (Bulletin of NASEN), Autumn.

Lorenz, S. (1998) *Effective In-Class Support: the Management of Support Staff in Mainstream and Special Schools*. London: David Fulton Publishers.

CHAPTER 3

Support and Self-esteem

Classroom support and self-esteem

When the first edition of this book was written, the role of the support teacher was a very new one. There were enormous self-esteem issues concerning the support teacher's relationship with the subject teacher. The feelings of students who were supported in class, and their parents also, was worth consideration. Making sure that students with special educational needs could access the curriculum in the same classroom as their more able peers was a new experience for all involved.

It is interesting to learn that now, a decade later, most of the same teachers see the support teacher in the classroom as an invaluable ally. It says much for the way in which teachers have absorbed the changes of ten years, which have placed tremendous demands on their resilience.

However, as explained in the previous chapter, support teachers have, for the most part, been replaced by teaching assistants (TAs). Where support teachers do exist they are often part of the central special services and do have expertise in special needs to offer. They have chosen their role as the second teacher in the classroom. Teachers, rather than being suspicious of their presence in the classroom, now plead for their presence when they are teaching certain classes.

Support teachers

In the early 1990s, being the second teacher in the classroom was a very new experience for the support teacher. As more children had been integrated into the mainstream and teaching teams from special schools had been redeployed, a number of these experienced teachers had found themselves supporting their previous clientele in mainstream classrooms. At that time support teachers were often teachers who had retired early from demanding and responsible positions or who were taking a break from full-time teaching to have more time to contribute to bringing up their own families. On returning to the same schools seven years later some of these teachers were found still to be in post. Often they had grown into the job and were the right hand assistant of the SENCO, taking considerable responsibility for Individual Educational Programmes (IEPs)and statement reviews. One spoke enthusiastically about her support of a succession of boys with Asperger syndrome who had been, or were going through, the school. She pointed out that although each boy had his own very individual personality, she felt that her experience had added to her confidence in acting as a consultant to other staff as well as a support to the students.

However, two of the support teachers to whom I spoke were dismayed that staff who had joined the school in recent years saw them as being unqualified classroom assistants and were reluctant to give them any responsibility. One spoke very bitterly of an incident on a school trip where the leader called over a Newly Qualified Teacher to take a group to another activity although she had volunteered to go. She was told that it had to be someone qualified.

Some qualified teachers with families had opted to be employed as Classroom Assistants, on a lower pay scale, as they did not feel able to devote as many hours to their work as they would have had to as teachers. In a situation where they were contracted to work in a less responsible role for less pay, it still rankled when they were treated as unqualified assistants. Schools that attracted trained teachers who wanted to work as classroom assistants were certainly gaining more than another pair of hands. Perhaps there should be some way of recognising that teachers who do not wish to work long hours have a value in a supporting role, and another teaching scale should be agreed acknowledging this.

The self-esteem of the support teacher

In the early 1980s the self-esteem of the support teacher was likely to take a daily battering, as described by this woman who had previously held a promoted post in a big primary school:

'I have been at my school two years now, but just this morning, when I was trying to persuade a boy to do something, he said to me "I don't have to do what you tell me. You're only a helper anyway." Look, I don't want to go about blowing my own trumpet and saying, "Look, I'm actually a very capable and qualified teacher", but I think we have got to do something about raising our status in the eyes of the children, and often in the eyes of our colleagues.'

Seven years later it appears that in many instances TAs who have received a similar response from a child have refused to accept this. Several spoke of reporting incidents to teachers or the SENCO, when pupils had spoken dismissively of them. Because of the novelty of the situation at first between the two teachers in the same classroom, I think the teacher used to often suffer in silence treatment to which a TA would certainly object.

Self-esteem is immeasurably increased in cases where subject teachers recognise the skills of the support teacher with whom they work and are ready to allow them to play a more satisfying role in the classroom. This kind of cooperation depends of course on the tact and the generosity of both teachers. Problems are most likely to arise where one, or both teachers, think that the only effective setting for learning is one where the children are silent and the teacher directs everything from the front of the room.

It is important that support teachers have an opportunity to meet together regularly and support each other. It is often in these sessions that they are able to value the work they have been doing. In one of the schools where I worked, I often coincided with a very self-effacing, elderly man, who I later learned was a retired headmaster. He was to be found quietly sitting beside some of the most disruptive pupils in the school, quietly encouraging them and sustaining them to finish tasks that earlier they had not had the confidence to attempt. Later, maybe because of his effectiveness in helping them to catch up with their peers, the funding for his pupils was discontinued and the SENCO organised a little ceremony for his pupils to say goodbye and thank you. At an INSET session, he shared with us his feelings about the tributes paid to him by these pupils: 'I found it overwhelming because of what they said. "Well, I said, is that me? Is that what I've been doing?"'

In common with many workers, it appears that support teachers are often only fully appreciated when they go. When support teachers meet together and share their concerns and anecdotes, they identify strongly with each other. Perhaps the best way to boost their self-esteem is to realise that if the time comes when they are no longer needed it probably means that they have been successful in helping those children to develop learning habits that enable them to be more independent, or they have given the class teachers enough confidence to feel that they can now cope with all the needs of the children in their classes.

The self-esteem of the subject teacher

Just as the support teacher is very dependent on the subject teacher for her own self-esteem, so she can do much to build the self-esteem of the subject teacher, or at least guard against diminishing the subject teacher's self esteem. Ever since the radical changes of the 1990s were mooted, teachers have been constantly criticised in the media for failing the children they teach. Yet the majority of teachers care intensely about their pupils and work hard to do their job as effectively as possible.

Nevertheless, it is easy for those outside the profession to point out that teachers rarely work for more than six weeks without a break, and finish their 'real work' before four o'clock. There is no other job where an employee has to face up to five different groups of 30 critical adolescents each day, and, week after week, hold their attention, energise them into producing increasingly prescribed work, enable them to work together in a constructive way, and constantly offer encouragement to those least likely to bring her credit. The teacher also has to make sure that there is enough order in the room to allow everyone to learn, even though some students might have no desire to cooperate, and none has actually chosen to be there. In most jobs, if employees feel a little below par they can reorganise their work to pace the day a little; but the good teacher has to show enthusiasm to deal with whatever is on the timetable for that slot, and needs to show as much animation last period on a Friday as any other time in the week.

Any one who has lived with adolescents will realise how critical they are of their teachers. Often, in trying to create their own identity, they are not just concerned with teaching style, effectiveness and discipline but also how their teachers look and dress, how they talk and their mannerisms and personality weaknesses. The responsibility of being a role model for many young people can put tremendous strain on any teacher, especially one who is only just gaining confidence in his or her new situation and work. A half-overheard remark of a child, or indeed a colleague, can undermine the confidence of a teacher. In these circumstances, is it surprising that subject teachers sometimes feel vulnerable when a second teacher is in the room, almost as an observer since he or she does not have the strain of preparing the lesson, does not have to settle the class down, and might not even have to do any marking?

It is very tempting for a support teacher to want to show the subject teacher that she is also a competent teacher with qualifications and experience. Much of the literature about support in the classroom talks about an interchangeable partnership, with the support teacher often taking the lesson while the subject teacher temporarily takes the subsidiary role.

My own view, however, is that because secondary school subject teachers are specialists it is totally valid that they should take the lead in the lesson unless the support teacher is also a specialist in the same area. In the most recent research, support teachers spoke, with great pleasure, of sometimes taking the main class while the subject teacher spent time with the special needs students, preparing them carefully for their course work This also boosts the self-esteem of the students who are sometimes sidelined in the classroom and left purely to the devices of the support teacher or teaching assistant.

Nevertheless the non-specialist support teacher, or teaching assistant, can have an invaluable role in the secondary school classroom, as discussed in the previous chapter. She can help the subject teacher to understand how the children learn by asking careful questions about the subject being taught. Indeed the non-specialist teacher may have the advantage of appreciating more easily the pupils' problems in understanding technical terms or unfamiliar words and phrases.

How, then, can the support staff play a significant role in the classroom without threatening the subject teacher's self-esteem? To begin with, the way in which questions are posed by the support staff to the specialist teacher is very important. It is only too easy to ask a question about the work that conveys the message that the subject teacher's explanation was poor to begin with. Young people, in pure self-defence, often ask questions in this manner, but it would be inexcusable for the support teacher to do this.

There are times when, even if the subject teacher's explanation has been understood, the support staff can ask for further explanation if they think that there are students who need a simpler explanation. This can avoid a situation where students are unable to start their work. It also show students how to ask politely for further help.

Another issue relates to the problem of giving support in lessons that are poorly taught. However often books, articles in journals and other professionals remind us that it is not the job of a support teacher to judge what goes on in the classroom, we would not be human if we truly did not notice. It is important, however, that we do not speak about what goes on in individual classrooms unless we feel that we are witnessing teaching that could corrupt or be harmful to students in the class.

Support teachers do sometimes find themselves in a situation where, week after week, they are sitting through lessons which fall apart to such an extent that there is little they can support. In such circumstances, there are two possible courses of action. One is to explain to your line manager that you do not feel your time is best spent in that lesson and leave the line manager to confirm that with the teacher. Some teachers in whose classes I have supported have welcomed this release from the pressure of having a second adult to witness their difficulties. However, the second course of action, which has been successful in a number of classes, has been to stay behind afterwards for a few minutes and talk about some part of the lesson which has gone well, or some action of the teacher which had made a real difference to a student. When present in such a lesson it is often possible to focus on tremendous strengths and care in some aspects of the interaction between the teacher and the class, despite other shortcomings. Often the teacher is surprised that you have noticed these skills as he or she may have been worried about the rest of the lesson. If the specialist is ready to acknowledge this, it is possible to discuss ways in which some of the class management could be split between the two of you to give the teacher more time to undertake the individual work he or she does best.

In one class I supported this is exactly what happened. The teacher was excellent at encouraging the weaker members of the class, but often lost the rest while he was doing this. We agreed that for six weeks, once he had started the class and explained what had to be done, I would manage the rest of the class and keep everyone on task so that he would have the opportunity to give quality time to individuals without worrying about the rest. In order to reach this stage I had to admit that I had had classes that had been a problem to me, and I suggested we experimented with this situation. By introducing ideas for the class with 'I wonder if…', he felt that he was making the decisions and I made sure that he told me what role he wanted me to play, even if I had sown the seeds of the idea. Because he then did not have to endure constant negative interactions with some of the more disruptive students, he was able to give them some of his valued individual attention. Gradually, with his permission, I started bringing in differentiated work cards so that those who finished quickly had a new challenge. This often involved finding information in reference books and on the computer, instead of engaging in idle chatter. The pupils earned appropriate credits and the noise level dropped sharply. It was important throughout, however, that the teacher was seen to be in charge and that my input was very much on a 'helper' level. At the end of the half term I had to move, but this young man was eager to report back to me his success with this class. He has shown me an excellent set of carefully differentiated work cards he made for the next topic and said how much some of the pupils have improved in their attitude to work. Had I instead waded in and tried to discipline the class and extend the brighter ones without his permission, I would have destroyed what little self-esteem he had at that point instead of building it. This was also a class with a number of students with learning and behavioural needs, found difficult by most of the staff. There is no guarantee that they would have behaved for me had I tried to override the teacher's discipline.

Of course, it is not always possible to work in this way and it requires generosity and trust from the subject teacher as well as tact from the support teacher. The general tactics, however, are clear enough. It is important for subject teachers' self-esteem that there is opportunity for them to share their concern about difficult pupils in a non-threatening situation.

Communication

The opportunity for communication between adults who work together in classrooms was seen as something absolutely necessary but lacking in 1993. In 2000 this was still not happening and was seen as one of the main problems with support in the classroom. This was where misunderstandings between adults sometimes occurred. It is important for the member of the team to share strategies that work with individual pupils, and cooperate in planning for individual children. They need to meet together regularly to do this and to evaluate the effectiveness of their planning. Well organised joint problem-solving meetings are useful in this context. These are described fully in Hanko (1985).

Problem-solving meetings

In this section I provide a description of how such a meeting works but I feel Hanko's book is necessary reading before implementing these groups. Before a joint problem-solving meeting is held, it is important to arrange a suitable time and to agree the length of meeting with all those who teach the student or students who are to be discussed. Since each meeting needs a commitment of teacher time it is important that the time required is known by all the participants and that the meeting begins and ends on time.

A meeting is best divided into three parts, with each part requiring about the same input of time. During the first part, everyone has the opportunity to give some information on the child. It must be established from the start that this is a confidential, professional meeting, so that hearsay (for example, about events at the child's home or at the youth club) might be contributed only as long as the source can be acknowledged, and, during the time allowed, any knowledge, however old, can be given. It is important during the first part of the meeting that teachers feel that they can report on how they find the student in their class, in a totally non-threatening setting. It is therefore probably better for members of the senior management team only to be present if they actually have day-to-day dealings with the student.

During the second part of the meeting, but not before other information about the student has been shared, everyone is invited to contribute details of any strategy which is effective on every occasion, or it might be the reporting of a device that engaged the student's interest in just one or two lessons, or even just where the student uncharacteristically smiled at the teacher or cooperated with another student in the class. During this part of the meeting, it is important to obtain as much positive feedback as possible about the student's reaction to the strategies tried. The teacher who has no trouble with him or her must try to remember what precisely it is that really engages this student's motivation, for it is that information which will be important to share with colleagues. The student's out of school pursuits and hobbies are relevant in this section, or in the first section. It is imporatant that neither of these sections overrun the time allocated, however much people want to say, as it is in the last section that a joint plan of action is made.

Everyone, with as much knowledge as possible of the child and of what has worked, will decide on realistic aims and agree a way forward. A scribe will be needed to record this plan, which will need to be read aloud, agreed and distributed to all members of the meeting as soon as possible. Before the time is up, the date and time of a follow-up meeting must be agreed. It is a good idea to have someone responsible for watching the clock so that there is no risk of running out of time before each section has achieved its aim. I have found these meetings successful and fairly popular with teachers. I think that by strictly regulating their length, one acknowledges the value of teachers' time. It is probably better to allow an hour per student initially, but the task can be done in 45 minutes once teachers are used to this way of working. The strict time limit means that the participants tend to be concise and prioritise what they say, often making sure that what is relevant to the meeting has been decided beforehand. A copy of the plan for the next few weeks can be given to the appropriate member of the senior management team.

The self-esteem of the pupil

Developing a pupil's self-esteem is possibly the most important single role of the support staff. When listening to support staff talking about their role as described in the previous chapter, the one generally successful aspect of the job they were able to define was their role in building the student's self-esteem. It is rarely acknowledged how many students in our schools suffer a form of depression that is linked inextricably with a failure to have confidence in their own value as a human being. The young people who give us most cause for anger and concern often fall into this category. As I started this book, a disturbing song, 'I'm Just a Teenage Dirtbag', was high in the pop charts! I think the video had a happy ending but the words were dire. As an adult it is difficult to remember what it was like to be a child and to have so little control over one's own life. This situation is even worse for children who are receiving mixed messages from the adults around them. On the one hand the adults themselves lack self-esteem because of long-term unemployment, their own educational failure, their existence on estates which are labelled 'sink estates' by the media. However, in fighting this feeling of rejection and anger, they often project themselves aggressively and claim to know more than the teachers and officials who from time to time try to negotiate with them.

In any class of 30 children, up to ten will be living in families which no longer contain both of their birth parents. Of these, four might well still be going through the effect of radical reorganisation, or disorganisation, of their lives at home. In a secondary school this might be the second time it has happened in the child's life. For many children school provides the only stability and certainty in their lives, and is certainly the safest place to offload some of the anger and despair they feel.

Sadly, we can rarely change the lives of the students once they leave school at the end of each day. However, support staff are in an unrivalled position to help these young people to understand some of the consequences of handling their depression inappropriately and causing more trouble for themselves at school. Many of the children we are asked to support, especially those with behavioural difficulties, will benefit from being helped to examine carefully the negative interactions they have with teachers. Support staff must be prepared to accept that once the child gains confidence in them they might start to share some of their problems with them. How this is handled will depend on the pastoral organisation of the school, but it will be important to show the student that you are interested in him or her as a person. Remember, there is often little anyone could, or indeed should, do to change a child's home life, but a child can feel good in knowing another adult who is ready to recognise his or her problems and feelings and to acknowledge the maturity he or she is showing in handling the situation. One of the advantages of being support staff is that the onus is not on one to settle the children at the start of the next lesson. If a stressed student talks to a subject teacher, however caring, the teacher usually has to rush on to the next class, but support staff often have some flexibility in this respect. An apology to the teacher of the next class is usually accepted as subject teachers are only too aware of the emotional needs of their students, which they do not have time to address.

Students who live in chaotic and stressful homes are often put under additional stress at school because of missing items of school uniform, PE gear and other equipment; since such things have low priority in home situations where the adults are still needing support. Support staff are in an ideal position to check with their protégées at the beginning of the day that they have these things. Sometimes they can lend spare items of equipment, or at least act as an advocate in smoothing the child's path with the staff who might later be reprimanding them about the missing items. Often the hardest-hearted head of year can be cajoled to lend a spare school tie or PE gear to a student who is struggling, against the odds, to conform to school requirements. The students who realise that they are worthy of this kind of special help from other adults not only have good role models but receive a boost to their self-esteem. It is important however, that this kind of help is given discreetly and the student does not feel patronised.

The support teacher also can often speak to students who are in constant trouble for not doing their homework. There are many reasons for adolescents being unable to do their homework in their own homes. It may be that such students, with the help of the support teacher, can be encouraged to negotiate with their teachers a time and place to complete this within school or they might be able to direct the child to one of the homework centres run by some LEAs. Since 1993 tremendous progress has been made in setting up study centres in schools, where help and support is available to students who genuinely want to do their homework but whose home conditions are difficult. This has been recognised, at government level, as an issue of equal opportunities and money has been spent of righting this wrong. However, there always have been students who rebel against doing homework, however good the conditions.

I was intrigued by two students who seemed quite content to be in detention every evening. Unknown to them, concern was expressed about their constant inclusion in the detention list and their teachers were asked to try to avoid putting them in detention for a few days. However, although the teachers duly turned a blind eye to some of their peccadillos, the pair still turned up for detention and pleaded to be allowed in, even to have it 'credited' to them for a later date! When asked why they wanted to be there, they said it was good because the teacher talked to you and helped you do your work, and sometimes you could get your homework done. These two streetwise 13-year-olds had tremendous need for individual attention even if they could only obtain it in negative mode.

Self-esteem and learning difficulties

Not all students who display inappropriate behaviour in class do so because of the stresses of their home lives. For many it is the stresses of their school lives that cause them to fight back with disruptive or disaffected behaviour. The self-esteem of a student with a book full of incomplete or shoddy work is often at rock bottom. Some students with moderate or specific learning difficulties have to suffer so many doubts and misgivings when they start a piece of work that, unless they are helped to overcome them, they will waste time and be disruptive. They will either spend ages writing, erasing and rewriting the date and the heading, or they will complete this stage and then avoid further commitment by finding, or creating, such distractions as a broken pencil, a leaking pen, a need to go to the lavatory or an engrossing conversation with a neighbour. The presence of support staff for these children is an absolute necessity if the subject teacher is to be able to engage the attention of the whole class.

The first piece of completed work in an exercise book gives a tremendous boost to the child's self-esteem. For that reason I think it is valid to provide more help than you would aim to do on subsequent occasions. At the same time it is easy to develop the habit of 'over helping' rather than patiently triggering the pupil to gradually take over more of the work. At secondary stage pupils are quite clear about what is actually their work and what the support teacher or assistant has done on their behalf. The feeling of being patronised will destroy any self-esteem that has been built up.

During the most recent research one 15-year-old girl spoke about being desperate for help but also being determined that the class would not connect the TA's presence in class with her needs. The TA had independently spoken of her frustration with this student who needed help but refused to accept it. This was a case where ingenuity was used to support the girl without harming her fragile self-esteem. The SENCO had actually arranged for her and two other very sensitive students to come to school for additional help at 8 o'clock in the morning. This had made a difference to the life of the whole family since their daughter's anger had been partly because of what was happening at school.

In a family with two girls, who were interviewed at home, the girls acknowledged that they could not survive without support but said that other students and youngsters on their estate taunted them and called them 'thickos'. Both girls had a reputation for being aggressive and loud. They admitted that this was a way of showing others that they did not care what they thought of them. Perhaps they were using this device to preserve their own self-esteem.

The next two chapters will deal with the different needs of those with moderate learning difficulties, and those with specific learning difficulties. However, it is relevant to point out at this stage that it is not always appropriate to expect the same work from each child in the class. The concept of differentiation in the classroom has always been with us but in recent years has been much more widely discussed and written about. Some secondary schools originally wrote into their policies that differentiation would be by output; that is, the same work would be given but each child would do it according to their own level. For this strategy to be successful the work has to be very carefully planned, to be open-ended and not necessarily insisting on a written response. The chances are that some teachers will set pieces of work that will be marked on set criteria, especially in these days of increased rigidity of attainment targets, etc., and it will be clear to the weaker students that they cannot succeed in the aims of the work. It is not sufficient for the teacher to tell them to draw a picture as an afterthought, or give them praise for their efforts at work they can see is not as good as that of others. There are now many more teachers in classrooms who have had INSET on differentiation, and who have trained since there was greater inclusion in mainstream classrooms. There are also far more published materials differentiating elements of the required curriculum. NASEN (the National Association of Special Educational Needs) is among a number of organisations and publishers who have produced useful materials. Some local authorities have produced such good materials that they are offered on the open market.

There are still situations where support staff have to use tact in order to find out about the planned lesson and to be able to come equipped with differentiated materials which will build the self-esteem of the student. However, the idea of inclusion has become embedded in the ethos of many schools, and there are now few teachers who do not welcome the help of support staff to empower students with learning difficulties.

Unfortunately it is still difficult to find times when subject teachers and support staff can meet to pre-plan what will happen in the lesson. This means that the support staff often work with a degree of uncertainty.

Body language

An important factor in building up the self-esteem of a secondary school student is in the body language we use when talking to him or her. I believe that with secondary school pupils you speak as adult to adult. If it is obvious that the young person does not understand words I am using, I repeat the statement again using more familiar vocabulary, but I never speak to a young person in a different tone or with less courtesy than I would speak to another adult. Some stress the importance of adults in charge of pupils assuming a physical presence that is dominant (Beynon 1985, Robertson 1981). For support staff, however, there is a danger that this practice could hinder much of the special work that they are able to contribute to building up the self-esteem of pupils. There are advantages in being in a position where you are not expected to establish dominance in order to control large numbers of unruly youngsters.

'The bag of chips'

When addressing teachers on INSET days about student self-esteem I often talk about the bag of chips that each child brings into school each day. I say child rather than student because this originates in the home. These are not potato chips but gambling chips, so it is a matter of luck how many you have. Some children leave home with a full bag of chips, but other have bags which start the day empty (Canfield and Wells 1976).

Each time a parent says or does something loving, kind or empowering to the child, a chip falls into the bag. This might be a goodnight kiss, for a small child a story, for the older child help with homework. It can also be things like knowing there is going to be a clean blouse or shirt to wear in the morning, knowing that there will be food for a packed lunch and anything else that is needed for the day. Chips also fall in the bag when children are listened to, praised, and sent off to school with good wishes for the day.

Unfortunately it is the very children who come into school with few, if any, chips in the bag, who begin to lose them as soon as they arrive at school. Chips are lost when something happens to make you feel bad inside. How often are students reprimanded for looking scruffy, not having dinner money, not coming to school prepared for the day. These are the very students who did not replenish their bag of chips the night before, and they end nearly every day at school either with an empty bag or in debt (some debts are paid off by detention, if a sensitive teacher uses this as an opportunity to talk to and listen to the detainees). It is the students who come into school with full bags who gain even more for handing in homework, looking smart and having a ready smile.

As far as self-esteem is concerned, unless in schools we try to reverse the process, the rich get richer and the poor get poorer.

Self-esteem and parents

The Government's Parent's Charter and the DfE Code of Practice say many fine words about the importance of parents as partners in their children's education. The revised Code of Practice (2000) puts even more emphasis on the role of parents in decisions regarding their children with special educational needs. For many parents, however, these words will remain mere rhetoric unless they can feel more comfortable when visiting the school. The reasons for parents behaving aggressively when visiting school is often similar to that of their children who behave aggressively in class until they begin to feel valued for themselves and for the work they do.

There has been a welcome change in policy by some schools which put as much stress on writing and telling parents when things are going well in school as they do when everything is going wrong and their offspring is about to be excluded. However, it is still more likely that most of the interactions that many parents have with schools are negative ones. These same parents may well still carry feelings of failure about their own schooling as many parents of children with learning and behavioural difficulties had similar problems themselves (Mason 1992). It is hardly surprising that some parents are so reluctant to put themselves in a position to have their fragile confidence undermined that they cannot even face coming to their child's statement review.

If the school agrees, some of support staff's time may be well spent establishing a working relationship with the parents of the child being supported. The support staff member is in such a close relationship with the child that the parents might well find it easier to talk to him or her rather than to the subject teachers or the Year head. I find it easiest, on the first visit, to give children I am supporting a lift home from school and let them introduce their parents to me. We are such important advocates for the children we support that it is important to give them the option of being in on this first meeting with their parents. Once the parents realise that you are on the side of their child it is usually easy to establish a rapport with them. They are also often happier about attending statement reviews if they know the support teacher will be there, and on the first occasion they might find it reassuring to be accompanied in the waiting room and to be seated near the support teacher during the meeting. If it is obvious that other professionals are speaking in jargon that excludes the parents, it is easier for the support teacher to request a 'translation'. If the parents views are being ignored or glossed over, it is important to draw attention to this fact.

For almost all parents it is an ordeal to sit in a formal meeting to discuss the problems of their child. Their enforced presence can only be justified if they are going to be listened to and their opinions valued and acknowledged. It is therefore important that they leave feeling that they had a full share in any decision made about their child's future. The meeting might have been a very humdrum, everyday event for most of the participants, but for the parents it might have been a major threat to their fragile self-esteem, especially if they have as children themselves or on behalf of other offspring been involved in any social services case conferences.

At the beginning of the 1990s a new element crept into the interaction between schools and some parents. Since the advent of league tables through which the academic performance of each school has been published in the media, senior management teams have felt a new vulnerability. This vulnerability is certainly affecting the relationship of schools with parents, especially parents of children with special educational needs.

The original Code of Practice was the instrument through which a child's special needs were identified, with the assumption being that the child would be given a place in the neighbourhood school. Fortunately the ethos of inclusion has improved to such an extent that most heads and their staff do not have a problem with this assumption. However, the Greenwich ruling (1981) and the formation of Grant Maintained, later Foundation Schools, with their own entry criteria, redefined what was meant by a neighbourhood school. At transfer to High School there was a myth that every parent had the right to choose the High School for their child. They would be helped in this by seeing which schools had done well in the league tables. Schools that were not chosen would simply close, while the 'good' schools would, just as simply, expand.

Needless to say, many of the most popular schools did not have the space to expand immediately so schools that were near the bottom of the tables had to remain open although, with the stigma of failure, few parents asked for them as first choice. During the early years of league tables one heard of pupils who could be relied upon to do well in their SATs (Statutory Attainment Tests) being offered two or three schools, while those who were lagging behind, often those with special educational needs, would not have a single offer until others decided which of the offers they were taking up. With attendance (or rather truancy) added to the equation there were parents who suffered the humiliation of knowing that their child was not wanted by any school in the area.

The situation of multiple offers of places arises because the LEA schools in a borough have one set of entry requirements, but each Foundation School has its own entry criteria. In places where there are Grammar Schools there is also a selection test . This meant that one child with good SATs and parents who presented themselves well at the promotional parents' evenings could end up in May with a place in a Grammar school, one in an LEA school and one in each of the other Foundation Schools. Unless parents of children with special needs put the lowest scoring of the schools down as first choice, it might be that no place could be allocated. In any system where there are winners there are, unfortunately, bound to be losers.

Self-esteem and the system

During the 1990s there developed an education system that is in danger of damaging the self-esteem of many teachers at all levels when their school is declared to be a 'failing' school after undergoing a two-week OFSTED experience. One can only imagine what effect this has on the self-esteem of whole families when a school, labelled as failing, is the only school to which their child can gain admission. Often it is the support staff who have to reach out to the children and their families and make them feel valued.

For students with a statement of educational need this exclusion issue has been addressed in the Code of Practice by giving parents the right to name the school that they prefer for their child. There is the understanding that if there is a place after other high-priority groups have been accepted the student with SEN must be offered a place.

In the revised Code of Practice there is to be additional emphasis on parents' rights to be involved in decisions about their children. This does not however redress the balance for those students who are on the special needs register but not statemented.

Conclusion

Self-esteem is the quality that makes people able to take on new challenges and gives them the confidence to make plans and have dreams. It is difficult to see how the past decade will be remembered as a time of educational progress if sections of the population are robbed of this investment in the future.

It is a credit to teachers that, despite having been attacked on all sides during the last decade, they have been so positive about the students with special needs in their classrooms. There is evidence in the classrooms of subject teachers, as well as support staff, being sensitive to the feelings of students who find work difficult. In a period when, at times, it seems that the requirement for higher and higher test results must weigh on teachers, most were still able to celebrate small steps forward with a child who was struggling.

The following chapters look at how the special learning styles of students with special needs can be addressed in the classroom.

Further reading

Canfield, H. and Wells J. D. (1976) *100 Ways of Enhancing Self-Esteem in the Classroom.* London: Prentice-Hall.

Hanko, G. (1985) *Supporting Special Needs in Ordinary Classrooms.* Oxford: Blackwell Education.

Hanko, G. (1999) *Increasing Competencies through Collaboration.* London: David Fulton.

CHAPTER 4

Supporting Students with Mild and Moderate Learning Difficulties

Prior to the 1981 Education Act, students who are the subject of this chapter would often have spent their entire schooldays in the segregated setting of a special school. These schools catered for students who were referred to as ESN (educationally subnormal); but the nomenclature of the 1980s, in an attempt to move away from the medical deficit model, renamed them schools for pupils with MLD (mild or moderate learning difficulties). Schools with the MLD label still exist, but it is unlikely that students who have only difficulty with learning will be in them. Most of the students now in these schools have behaviour, social or emotional difficulties also. The majority of students who have an overall mild or moderate learning difficulty are in mainstream schools.

In the secondary school, support staff will largely be dealing with those students who have struggled unsuccessfully all their lives to keep up with their classmates, but have never drawn so much attention to themselves that their teachers have insisted on their removal to a segregated setting. Since the 1981 Education Act there has been a marked reluctance to send any student to a special school unless they are adversely affecting the education of others in their class, or are themselves showing signs of unhappiness. In 1993 there were quite a few students in secondary schools who had spent much of their earlier school life in a special school and were in the process of being reintegrated back into mainstream. Now there are few students who have spent their primary years in a special school. During the first research project the inclusion of students with Down's syndrome was rare. Now the parents rarely have to battle to procure a place for their child in a mainstream primary school. An increasing number of secondary schools are now accepting Down's syndrome students, but some still have reservations. This progress has been due not only to changes in legislation, but also the determination of parents and the pressure group supporting them (see Appendix, and Further reading).

Unfortunately, because of their struggles throughout primary schools, some of these students will have low expectations of their ability to succeed and might have already developed all kinds of strategies to divert attention from themselves and their work. There will however be some who have received good 1:1 teaching and plenty of support and might well have experienced exceptional success in a sometimes segregated but sympathetic setting. They are often eager to join in with the class as they will have been used to having attention from the teacher. All these students need a great deal of support, and attention to the differentiation of their work. Unlike the situation in primary school, they no longer have one teacher who understands them, and has often watched them growing up through the school. The continuity and quality of support is of paramount importance, but it is essential that they do not just become the responsibility of support staff.

A well-meaning independent school prides itself on giving a place in every form to a local child with Down's syndrome, or some other learning difficulty. Parents of the other children are reminded to include this child in parties and outings. The other pupils really do include these children in their games. However, there is a nursery nurse attached to each of these children, and it is she who teaches them in the classroom, often seated between the child and the rest of the class. It is so important that the subject teacher is involved in the education of each student in the group, however good the support staff.

The aims of inclusion

Even now, almost a quarter of a century since the deliberations recorded in the Warnock Report (DES 1978) and twenty years since the implementation of the 1981 Education Act, it is interesting to reflect on the aims of integration since this has implications for support strategies. At that time we referred to integration as the returning to mainstream of those who since the 1944 Act had often been segregated in special schools and units.

Inclusion is the term more often used now, since the planning must be for all to be included in mainstream. Few teachers who have qualified in the last 20 years would be comfortable with the concept of students being denied all contact with their 'normal' peers because they had a difficulty in aspects of their physical, sensory or cognitive development. The move to integrate all students into mainstream and to provide individually planned compensation for their needs in that context was rightly seen as a step, if not a giant stride, in the right direction. The logical accompaniment to this was the move to make it more difficult to segregate children to start with. The former Special Education (SE) forms that were filled in when teachers felt a student would be better catered for in a special school were replaced by the 'Warnock stages', where a process was begun to formulate what extra intervention was required in order for the student to have equal access to the curriculum in mainstream.

Sixteen years after the publication of the Warnock Report, the 'Code of Practice' from the DfE (1994) defined the stages in the identification and assessment of special needs very clearly. The aim in 1981, as it is today, was to make the curriculum accessible to all children. There have always been some aspects of the curriculum which need to be modified for students with special needs, if they were to be allowed to learn at a suitable pace for themselves and if they were to have some feelings of success. The concept of 'differentiation' of teaching materials became all-important as teachers realised that mixed ability teaching was expanding its boundaries at both ends, but particularly at the lower end.

The intention was that difficulties in learning should not isolate a child from neighbourhood friendship groups and the opportunity to participate in the full range of subjects in the curriculum. They should also have access to all social and sporting activities offered by the local school. During the early and mid-1980s the practical aim in secondary schools was often to reintegrate those students who had been in segregated provision during primary school years. These were students who had often experienced considerable success in a segregated setting and were believed to be able to cope with the social aspect of mainstream life. The first students to be reintegrated were often the students whose parents had been vociferous in wanting this for their children and were therefore very supportive of the school as well as the child. Because of experience of success and of parental support, these students often did very well.

As LEAs closed their special schools and used the experienced staff as integration teams, schools with a high teacher–pupil ratio were no longer an option. In 1993 the research looked at the integration of these students. Seven years later we are seeing inclusion, the pace and success of which has surprised many who doubted its feasibility. There is however, still an issue about whether sufficient resources have been placed in schools to cater for the needs of these students. The system has been 'baled out' by the readiness of an army of Teaching Assistants (TAs) to provide support in the classroom. This leads to concern about a situation in which the education of the very students who are most in need of skilled teaching is often handed over to unqualified staff. If TAs were to have statutory training in special educational needs, and a proper career structure, would schools still be able to afford them?

If all students are to benefit from inclusion it is important that good systems of support are in place, and that there is a sufficient budget to provide for this. If students have had time in a special school or unit it is particularly important that they are phased into mainstream with the help of familiar staff. In the early 1990s thoughtful and elaborate plans were often made to integrate individual students, but as soon as the process seemed to be going well the 'bridge' from the special school was pulled away. There were cases where students survived a honeymoon period but then faltered. In one case the student became socially isolated and developed emotional and behavioural difficulties, which eventually led her to drop out of school altogether. Support for students with considerable learning difficulties is often most needed before and after school and during breaktimes, when these students often become the victims of bullies (Barrett and Jones 1996). Because of language difficulties and because of poor self-esteem these vulnerable students often feel unable to enlist help. In the recent research one girl said of her experience of bullying:

> 'They take the piss out of my teeth. Look, I've got frames [braces] up here. They call me donkey. Someone has punched me before. Someone has slapped me round the face. There are some girls and they have got a group and they like just come over to me and are horrible. I don't like telling the teachers about bullying. I don't like my mum phoning up the school because when they find out and when I go to school I am going to get more bullied than I am … It was worse in Year 7 because I would argue back at them.'

This was a girl who had sustained brain damage at 20 months when she had her first epileptic seizure. Her epilepsy was eventually brought under control, but not until she was four. Her sister, who is just about to transfer to the same secondary school, also has special needs. She said:

> 'Everybody takes the mickey out of you if you need extra help. They say we're "thickies". I don't take any notice but I am a bit scared about going to secondary school. All people at my school say scarey things about it. They say you can get killed there. They say there is a tree there and they throw your bag up there.'

Successful inclusion

If one of the aims of inclusion is to increase social opportunities, we must look at the students and see if they are part of the kind of friendship group that most children enjoy. If they are isolated in the playground, or the butt of jokes and always the fall guys in playground games, perhaps support in the playground is needed for inclusion to be successful. In two schools visited recently, TAs had non-contact time during some lessons in order to be able to support vulnerable students in the playground. The TAs were sometimes in the position to initiate a game where the special needs students could be included, but that other students would also enjoy. Again, very often if the situation is right for the student with special needs other students gain also.

In another boys' school, two TAs ran a lunch-time ABC club (All Busy Club) where students could get help with their homework or project work. If students are unable to join in any lesson without adult support, the situation has to be scrutinised in case it is making the student over-dependent rather than encouraging independence. In some schools there is a policy of allocating a group of students with similar needs to a TA, and then leaving the TA to interpret the lesson to them. The message here can be that there is no onus on the students to listen to the lesson as the TA will make sure that they know the essentials. It is important that the subject teacher is as involved in the learning of these students as that of any other students. It is the teacher who has had professional training in pedagogy. Although teachers are under more pressure than ever before, it is still up to the teachers to decide that if the students are not learning as a result of the way they are teaching them then they must explore ways of teaching so that the student can learn. There should be opportunities to discuss strategies with colleagues who are succeeding.

Challenges to inclusion

There are however some students with special needs who resent the attention of support staff. A 15-year-old girl interviewed recently admitted that the support staff had always been ready to give her help but she would rather fail than be seen to need help. She covered up her difficulties by misbehaving so that peers believed that her work was unfinished and poor because she was not listening and did not try, rather than that she could not do it unaided.

There was a similar student who was one of the first boys integrated from the local MLD school in 1993. Kevin had elderly foster parents who had cared for him since he was a toddler and were very supportive of whatever the professionals thought was best for Kevin. They attended all meetings with him and were quick to respond to the school when Kevin truanted on two occasions with another boy in his class. Kevin has a lot of difficulty with his work but will not tolerate the help of support staff. It was therefore necessary to locate another student, close to Kevin, who was doing similar work and speak to that student about the work in a voice loud enough to reach Kevin. Kevin was then in a position to chose whether he accepted help or not, and was often seen to listen intently and then act upon the teaching he had heard.

However, he often submitted work that was unfinished and which was inferior to some of the neat, but less demanding work, that he did at his special school. He sat with a group of the class reprobates and joined in the passing of notes and risqué pictures with them during lessons. He often found himself in detention at the end of the day, but he had managed to gain a place in the house football team and was a reserve for the under 15 Second XI. His foster parents were disappointed that he did not join any afterschool clubs. However, he was far more integrated into the group than those who accepted more support.

In contrast Haley, aged 12 years, went to the same school as Kevin from the age of 8 until she was 11, but was transferred to her original primary school for just one term before secondary school transfer. The staff of this school were not happy about her integration as no funds were available to give her the help she needed. There was also a dispute between her parents. Her mother wanted her to transfer to a very big secondary school, whereas the professionals recommended a smaller school. Her father agreed with the professionals' judgement. Although the mother refused to visit the second school, a place was offered and accepted by the father. Hayley started there in September.

Hayley read well, better than many of her class, but with very little understanding. She wrote very neatly but her work was repetitious and uncreative. She knew most of her multiplication tables and could add and take away as competently as many in her class. With an IQ of 92 she was an ideal case for integration but she spent most of her time wandering round on her own. She was frequently in tears and made a beeline for any adult who approached. In a PE lesson she would stand helplessly after any activity, waiting for her group to reclaim her. When being supported in lessons she frequently complained of feeling tired, and if made to persevere with a task she either demanded to be allowed to go to the lavatory or simply burst into tears. She was always eager for support staff to sit next to her and would resent any other student who asked for help.

Hayley has a higher IQ than Kevin and was integrated at an earlier age, but the integration had not in any way succeeded. She became unhappy and had begun to refuse to go to school, and her parents' conflicts over her education made it difficult for them to support her in her school. In these two cases Kevin was included completely with his peers, whereas Hayley's integration was purely locational. Even now, at a time when there is evidence of great strides having been made towards inclusion in most schools, there are still some students who are in the school but not of the school. If they spend a substantial part of their days 'velcroed' to an adult, they will stay this way, and yet support is needed.

Accepting differences

In secondary schools, in 1993, we had some students who, pre-Warnock, would have received segregated education from an early stage of their primary schooling. However, many of these students started in mainstream and remained there throughout their school careers. Most of the time they caused concern to their teachers because of their inability to match the progress of the rest of the class, and the gap between their performance and that of their peers had become more obvious by the time that they had reached secondary school. Peter, and his twin Paul, were two such students. They were born prematurely into a large and loving family. They were 14 years old in 1993 and they were often in the same lessons. Peter's work was untidy and badly written and he relied greatly on the girl beside whom he was sitting, often copying her work, word for word. In contrast, Paul's work was immaculately tidy and well written but he also relied a great deal upon the girl next to him. Both boys were very popular with the girls as they were nice looking and took a great pride in their appearance and their personal freshness.

Although Peter had more independence in spelling and working out his own calculations, teachers tended to perceive Paul as being brighter as his work was always well presented. There was much good natured rivalry between the boys, and one of the girls remarked that 'although Paul is cuter, Peter is more of a laugh'. They both looked forward to leaving school and joining the family building firm. The staff were split between demanding that they be moved to a more suitable school (i.e. an MLD School) before Year 10, and acknowledged that they were just as well where they were. They were entirely honest about their need to copy the work of other students, and acknowledged that they chose their helpers well. This dependence on their classmates in no way diminished their social standing among their peers. They had all grown up together. However, they would not boost their school's performance in the league tables at the end of Year 11. Fortunately it was a large school so their results would not have made as much difference as if they had been two per cent of a Year 11 with only 100 pupils.

When even support is not enough

Jason was also 14, the younger of two brothers, both of whom had needed in-class support. An undersized boy with very dry hair that refused to lie flat against his head, he was nicknamed 'Peanut' by most of his Year group, and indeed many of the other children in the playground. When asked if he enjoyed having a nickname he was quite definite about his dislike of being called by this name. Despite the fact that the deputy head had asked staff to reprimand pupils who called Jason by this nickname, teachers were heard to use this name.

Jason stood out in the classroom as a student who was unable to join in with the lesson in any way. While the teacher was writing on the board the other students removed his rubber and ruler and forced him to beg for their return. As they left the classroom a boy, who claimed to be his friend, let his bag swing in Jason's face. In the next lesson (RE) Jason was the only student who did not at any time join in the animated discussion on Easter customs, despite the teacher's sensitive attempts to ask him about hot cross buns or Easter eggs. Only when he was withdrawn for lessons was he able to make any headway with his work. His progress was painfully slow but he was happy to be away from the class, and his parents requested that this should happen more often. After discussions with his parents and other concerned professionals, it was decided that Jason was not benefiting from remaining in mainstream and would profit from a bridging course at the MLD school. This was to ease the passage from school to a Further Education college. Jason transferred the Easter before Year 10 and managed to make friends with two boys and a girl in his class. They did not use school transport and did the daily journey by bus. They were often seen sitting on a seat, deep in conversation, in one of the shopping parades in the borough where they had to change buses.

The above two examples demonstrate another set of contrasting experiences. Again, the aims of inclusion were satisfied in one case but not the other; although it is possible that Peter and Paul would have benefited from a different teaching approach at a special school, socially they gained from inclusion. The aim must be to provide quality and quantity of support to students like this. With TAs, schools can afford quantity, but they must make sure that this is of the highest quality possible. For inclusion to work, the traditional attitudes and expectations of teachers have had to change as much as those of children and their parents. Dessent (1987: 85) warned:

> Expertise in special needs is often more to do with knowing what cannot be done than knowing what can be done. Living with educational failure and making appropriate teaching adjustments to

redefine what counts as 'success', is at the end of the day, what expertise in special needs is about.

He continues:

> Support services in ordinary schools have rarely addressed the issue of educational failure. They have traditionally operated on a 'success' or 'curative' model ... if children with special needs are to be educated appropriately within mainstream education then a major requirement must be that mainstream teachers learn to live with the relative 'failure' of pupils in traditional educational skills.

This was written before 'league tables' became a reality! In a large school it is possible to celebrate Ds, Es and Fs, but in a small school results that are a triumph for students with special needs can cost places in the overall results for a school.

How can inclusion fail special students?

The Audit Commission (1992) had focused on concerns about how monies intended to implement successful integration had been allowed to drift in schools because of lack of accountability. Without the deliberate grouping of students with SEN around a student with a statement, there would be little help for those students on Levels 2 and 3 of the Code of Practice. Much more time and energy would also be used trying to obtain statements of special need for more students. There are also some special needs teachers who are reluctant to stigmatise a student by asking support staff to work specifically with an individual student, and so support is put into the classroom on a very general basis for the benefit of all the students. Occasionally support staff, who are regularly working in classrooms and are paid with money which is attached to a statement, do not know which of the students they are supporting is the one with the statement. They will be working from the student's Individual Education Plan (IEP).

Adults are often more sensitive to the feelings of students with special needs than is necessary. If a student's needs are such that they need to have a formal statement it is likely that others in the class will be well aware of their difficulties. During the course of my research two students spoke strongly about this. Kieran said:

> Sometimes people are embarrassed about having a support teacher, but often they are embarrassed about not being able to read and having to go up to the teacher and ask all the time ... The teacher is there to help me, but there is someone else in the classroom who has absolutely no

need whatsoever, who thinks, there's another teacher in the classroom …I might as well make life easier for myself as well… I don't think it's fair when the person can get on perfectly well without him or her. (Y9 boy 1993)

A girl with cerebral palsy spoke of the support assistance provided for her in a needlework lesson:

It is so frustrating. It takes me ages to thread a needle. I cannot hold my right hand high enough to be able to see the eye, and then my left hand shakes so much… but I am not so good at attracting attention as others, so often the support is busy helping the shouters, and I get into trouble because I have not started. I cannot start until my needle is threaded for me. (Y9 girl 2000)

Nevertheless there were students who did not want to seem to obviously need help:

I know I need help but I don't want it to be obvious. If a support teacher helps me I like the others to think it's because she likes me. (Y 9 boy 1993)

I know I need help but I would rather not have it than for the others to know. I know that I am my own worse enemy over this. Now I can come in and have help before school, I will do that. (Y10 girl 2000)

However, Year 7 students could not see any link between being supported and being embarrassed. They had often been supported throughout their primary school years. In their early years at secondary school students with MLD seem to have few reservations about being helped by a second adult in the room. Most of the students are friendly and welcome the extra support. One girl said:

I know I need a lot of help, and it is good when I know that, as soon as the others are working, the teacher will come and check with me. That happens in English and Geography lessons. In other lessons I sometimes have to shout for help. (Y10 girl 2000)

Support staff allocated to a particular child should be familiar with the recommendations on the statement, and concentrate on finding ways to implement these. Often the aims written on the statement are completely different from those of the teacher, but support staff are there to serve the teacher as well as the student. Perhaps the teacher has decided that a certain piece of work must be finished before half term. This can cause conflict for the person who is supporting a student who is able to write neatly and correctly, and is very eager to please, especially the teacher. However, he does not actually understand the processes about which he is going to write. Educationally, the support staff should go over it again with him, using different vocabulary and slowing down at some points for him to grasp the meaning, but this would mean the piece of work would not be ready to be submitted at the end of the lesson. In cases like these it is necessary to give him a lot of help with the work, even writing it out for him to copy, and he will have the satisfaction of giving in a neat, praiseworthy piece of work, like everyone else at the end of the lesson. It is essential that this is recorded as this topic will need extra revision in the run-up to examinations.

On one level this has been a valid activity as the student has been seen to be included in the class. He has also been praised for neat work in front of the class, but one child has remarked loudly that he has had a lot of help from the support staff. On another level he is reaching that point in Science lessons when it is less likely that he will be able to grasp the concepts, that several others are also finding very difficult. Perhaps the experience of being part of a group is as important as learning on a level that he can understand?

It is important for teachers and support staff to consider the priorities when preparing SEN students for examinations. There is now greater awareness that the GCSE is not the ideal examination for all students, and sometimes other routes need to be explored. The foundation stages of the GNVQ are often manageable steps to obtaining a nationally recognised qualification. Some students between the ages of 14 and 19 will now be supported at the local FE college as this is an option in some authorities where adolescents with learning difficulties have become disaffected, and might benefit from a new start. They will have access to those qualifications which allow for recognition of practical ability in numeracy and literacy, as well as skill in vocational subjects. Nevertheless, this curriculum alone does not always obviate the need for good support. The support role in FE colleges is very important as pressure from demotivated peers can easily be greater than the pressure from overstretched lecturers, in matters such as attendance and submission of work. The cognitive support is also important. For this reason it is very important that training in special needs teaching, and understanding, is available to and undertaken by lecturers and instructors in FE colleges. It is short-sighted to see FE colleges as the solution to disaffection in schools if this is not in place.

The change to support teaching from the teaching of special groups of 'remedial' students who proceeded up the school, cocooned with their kindly teacher in 'the hut', is now complete. However, these students still have the need to be taught some subjects or topics at a pace at which they can succeed. Unfortunately, some of the areas of school life where they could excel have now been replaced with other subjects. For example, Food

Technology, with its emphasis on process and experimentation, does not give the slow learner the same opportunity for tangible success as its predecessor, Home Economics. In this lesson the product was important and a plate of uniformly jammy tarts could be passed round the group. Perhaps the resurgence of parenting classes will give this group the opportunity to really engage in a subject.

Although this dates back a number of years I still like the idea of a support workshop described in Bell and Best (1986). I have only seen it in action in one school; a school that had the courage to use a full-time teacher and a fairly central room for this initiative.

> A room has been prepared with individual work carrels and stocked with teaching machines [these have now been replaced with all purpose computers] language consoles, cassette recorders, reading schemes, problem-solving materials, spelling programmes, numeracy games, sets of comprehension exercises, extension work and so on ... to minimise the disruption in the child's classroom work, the workshop session itself runs for no longer than 15 minutes, the children leaving their normal classroom to discuss their progress and collect the next instalment of material aimed at developing a specific skill. Obviously these arrangements are not made on an ad hoc basis and negotiation has to take place between the class teacher and the support teacher to agree the most suitable and convenient time for children to attend these short sessions. (Bell and Best: 102)

In several schools an experienced teacher spent specified periods each week in the school resource centre, where students were helped 'by appointment'. However, this concept was marred by the fact that disruptive students were often also sent there ad hoc. One school used the resource centre for a homework club, but students with special needs went there for afterschool programmes. Because they selected themselves to make use of this facility they did not feel stigmatised. There were a number of ambitious students who preferred to use the club than try to work at home with background noise. Because it was in the library, books were readily available and there was plenty of room.

There are a number of advantages in this kind of arrangement. The very clever student in the class may well go along before or after the one with learning difficulties, since extension work as well as remedial work is based in this room. A student whose only problem is his handwriting is as likely to be booked in for a workshop session as the child who needs help in understanding basic concepts. It is also very good use of the support teacher's time and expertise, as she would be constantly engaged in planning for children and interacting with them, rather than sometimes sitting and listening to a lesson, unable to intervene or plan in any way. On the other hand the student is only being withdrawn for a specific time, and with a specified, well-defined aim, and will shortly be returning to mainstream provision.

There are a number of examples of excellent resource rooms, but, with personpower cut back to the bone, it is difficult to maintain the possibility for students to have a 15-minute individually tailored input for their needs.

Making support successful

Making support successful is a very important responsibility of subject teachers and support staff. This is even more so when children know that the support is directed at them and not just generally available in the classroom, as the following example illustrates.

Billy flatly refused to accept any support. He would put his arms protectively around his work and refuse to let any support teacher see what he was doing. Often he had nothing to hand in at the end of the lesson. The teacher invariably asked support staff to help Billy, and was understandably frustrated when no one did. On investigating this case, it emerged that Billy had accepted support in lower forms but had still found his work difficult because he had quite severe learning problems. Other children had pointed out that even with support he had not done well. He now seemed to have decided that it was worse to fail with support than on your own!

Perhaps if there had been more time for teachers to confer, Billy could have done a different piece of achievable work, which would have been both acceptable to the teacher, and within his grasp, so that he would have had a successful outcome. One of the great difficulties with supporting pupils in secondary schools is the lack of time and opportunity for teachers and support staff to confer together about individual pupils and their needs. It is also sometimes difficult for support staff to devise work in a subject in which they do not have specialist knowledge. It is important for support staff to do all they can to secure liaison if support is to be as effective as it can be. In the above case, input as well as output, should have been negotiated early on so that Billy was not left with a sense of failure. There is a big problem when subject teachers allow themselves to believe that a student with SEN plus support miraculously becomes a student without SEN!

It seems obvious to say that the route to good support is through effective differentiation. Unfortunately, experts who glibly talk about differentiation often find it difficult to give practical examples in the secondary school. It is easy to state, as has been done in some SEN policies, that 'differentiation by outcome is available throughout the school'. This hardly needs stating: of course different students give in the work complete or incomplete, well done or not so well done! The key question, however, is how does the student whose work is differentiated by outcome feel when he does not have one complete piece of work in his book? Would it not be better to offer differentiated or sequenced activities?

Some of the newer textbooks have activities at the end of each chapter which are graded in difficulty so that everyone in the class can complete the first one or two with some element of success, and the abler pupils will complete further exercises with a gradual increase of effort and the use of resources such as reference books, atlases and dictionaries. These kinds of differentiated activities are definitely worth looking for when deciding on the purchase of new textbooks. If the textbook does not offer these exercises I favour sets of 'home-made' work cards that are linked to the specific lesson being taught. If the support staff have the opportunity to liaise regularly with the subject teacher, they can produce these. I use box filing cards, colour-coded according to difficulty. When teaching mixed ability groups for modern foreign languages a box of cards was prepared for each module of the course. These were laminated so that they could be taken home for homework. While giving out homework I knew by the colour, at a glance, which card to give. Each card was numbered so that there was a variety of activities at each level that would consolidate the learning according to the student's ability. If it was a listening exercise the tape would have a sticker of the same colour with the corresponding card number on it. The cards were often used in class and cassette recorders were available for students to privately record their sentences until they were satisfied.

Each of these cards should require one complete, achievable task to be done. Some tasks can be drawing or copying, and some might be oral or aural. While providing success for those with learning difficulties, this also provides extension exercises for those who are very able. If the class is engaged in working on a variety of activities which are germane to the lesson, the teachers have time to listen and help with the oral work, which will offer a good indication of how much of each topic has been understood and internalised.

Another method of providing differentiation is to produce a wall newspaper of the topic being covered. With this method, the brightest pupils can be given the more demanding tasks, requiring a certain amount of research, whereas the slower learners can be given tasks that consolidate that which they are able to grasp. This could be filling in the missing words in a short article written by the teacher, or being part of a small group making up a wordsearch using all the most important terms, making up a simple crossword, copying a map or diagram, asking one of the teachers a list of questions and writing down the answers in the form of an interview. It might be possible to use the computer to produce an edition that can be taken home. Because groups of children will produce items between them, everyone should be able to see an item with their name under it.

Both these interventions are dependent on the subject teacher being willing to work in partnership with support staff. Where there is little communication between the two adults, either because of time constraints, or differences in philosophy, it can still be possible to give effective support. Sometimes the most useful support is to encourage the students to think about what they are doing, and why. Very often the kind of conversations that parents and grandparents have with little children transfer well to this situation. This is recognised by those who have studied 'thinking skills', also known as 'meta-cognition', which is basically, 'thinking about thinking'.

Thinking about thinking

Reuven Feuerstein is an Israeli psychologist who was concerned about children who seemed to find it difficult to learn by experience. He encountered recently immigrated children who were either haphazard and impulsive in their responses, or were passive and inert when faced with a new challenge. He refused to believe that this was lack of intelligence and instead assumed that they had never learnt to structure their thinking. To remedy this, he devised a set of activities, or 'instruments', which were designed to exercise specific areas of the brain. Hence the method became known as 'Instrumental Enrichment'.

A very important aspect of this method is that it must only be used by people trained in the method. This is considered vital as an essential part of the process is that the child should be talked through each stage. The first instrument, for example, entails placing joining lines through what seem to be random series of dots in order to produce a set group of geometrical figures which overlap differently at each stage. As much emphasis is placed on the relating of each activity to other subjects in the curriculum, as is put on the process of completing the actual instrument. The term which describes relating the processes to the curriculum and to everyday tasks is known as 'bridging'.

Few support staff will have the time or resources to become trained instrumental enrichment tutors, but all can benefit from being conscious of the importance of bridging, whatever the activity. For those who would like more information there are addresses in the Appendix. In 1988, a Somerset educational psychologist, Nigel Blagg, compiled a course of thinking skills based on instrumental enrichment and the 'Philosophy for Children' method pioneered by Matthew Lipmann (1991). These are available as a series of five books of affordable photocopiable sheets.

The role of the teacher or support staff in meta-cognition is 'mediating' learning. The key characteristic of 'mediated' learning is to help the child grasp the teachers' intentions. One of the areas that lends itself well to this intervention is the Technology lesson. As the second adult in the room the support staff member can look carefully at materials with the student, and ponder on why the specialist teacher is using those materials rather than others, or why this task is being set. However, it is possible to do this in other lessons, or even in those moments before and after a lesson when nothing constructive is happening. Support staff who are asked to take part in school trips have an excellent opportunity to focus individual students on new stimuli and talk through their perceptions.

The important aim of the mediation is that the student should not be the passive recipient of learning or of experiences. 'Now I wonder what Mr Brown wants to see in your exercise book', will develop the student's thinking more than, 'Now did you understand that, Mr Brown wants you to...'. 'What do you think Mr Brown will think when he sees this?', is more likely to establish a habit of self-evaluation than, 'Come on, read this through before you give it in'.

All Feuerstein's Instruments have on the front page a picture of a child who could be a boy or a girl. The child is obviously wrestling with a problem and the words, 'Just a minute. Let me think.' are on this page. I supported a girl who was of low intelligence but desperate to keep up with the rest of the class. She was very impulsive and often started her work before the teacher had finished giving the instructions so that she would not get behind. Consequently her marks were disappointing and by the time I was called in she was presenting with behavioural problems. I had six individual sessions with her during which we completed the first instrument and part of the second instrument. She learnt to listen to the teacher, by assuming the pose of the child on the instrument and saying to herself, 'Just a minute. Let me think.' She followed these instructions excellently, and, despite substituting, 'Ang on. I got to fink abaht it', for the recognised formula, her work improved noticeably, as did her self-esteem.

One of the main strengths of any course of thinking skills is in improving the student's self-esteem, as well as enhancing the ability to learn. The Somerset Thinking Skills Scheme mentioned earlier aims to do this by:

- the use of a large range of discussion/problem-solving;
- tasks that are relatively free from previous failure experience;
- the inclusion of open-ended tasks where there are many alternative, justifiable interpretations, communicating to the pupils that the teacher is not necessarily looking for one correct answer;
- the provision of interesting visuals to stimulate and extend pupil ideas and provide a learning environment that presents tasks in multiple modes;
- the careful sequencing of pupil activities to enable pupils to reinforce and build on basic skills, resources and strategies;
- the emphasis on small group work, enabling pupils to help one another, comparing, sharing and reflecting on skills;
- procedures and solutions.

There are groups of professionals meeting in many areas to share their interest in the role of thinking skills, or meta-cognition, in education. It certainly has a place in the support of special educational needs in mainstream schools. A short period of carefully guided work on thinking skills a couple of times a week would enhance the performance of students in a class. However the thinking skills exercises or instruments need careful delivery if they are to achieve their full potential and are certainly not to be seen as being an easy option for giving out to students to occupy them during registration/form time. The adult mediation of the experience is essential.

How do we measure success

It is difficult to define success with those children who will never totally catch up with their peers in a society which sees examination results as the main indicator of success. However, it is possible to call to mind such pupils who bear more evidence of their success after school than do many of their brighter peers. I recently met a young man who was the most limited pupil I ever taught in a unit for disruptive pupils. He was the seventh of eight children whose mother had died when he was five, and whose father was disabled. He had become disruptive in his special school when he had ceased to make any progress after the age of fourteen. He was a very, very angry adolescent and totally refused to make any effort with school work. He had a talent for copying pictures very accurately and could often be persuaded to copy something about the picture under it. He liked to know what it said and took the trouble to memorise whatever he had written. I am afraid this was the extent of our success with Matthew's literacy skills.

However, on a group trip to a local Youth Hostel in the countryside, he became a leader. His special school had been in the country, and he knew all about closing gates, climbing stiles, recognising trees by their leaves and nuts, and he could see which sheep were about to lamb and which already had. He was a different, delightful boy and we were not surprised when the warden invited him to visit the following weekend to help with a younger party.

Matthew at 23 was engaged to a girl he had met during his many weekends at the Youth Hostel. They are both ardent conservationists. He has learnt to read and has enough confidence to stand up and speak at meetings. Above all, he is happy and proud of his life. He describes some of his fellow pupils as losers because they have been in trouble with the law. He obviously sees himself as a winner.

Although not every young person has access to this kind of success, I am sure many readers will call to mind similar stories. It is important that when we support students with learning difficulties, we recognise when they can go no further with literacy and numeracy, for the time being, and give them the opportunity to succeed in other ways. By the age of 14 these students have often exhausted all the different approaches to teaching literacy. There is a very narrow path to tread between under-extending such students, and pushing them so hard that they have to resort to distracting behaviour in order to survive. Materials used must be motivating to the individual. All children have now been taught a common National Curriculum since starting school, however there is still the possibility, with a well written Individual Education Plan (IEP), to reach targets using materials that motivate the student. It is worth bearing in mind that, unless one is going to become an academic or a writer, one is much more likely to use the spoken rather than the written word.

At a parents' evening a colleague was feeling considerable trepidation at the prospect of telling a girl's parents how little progress she had made in learning to read. The parents had not visited the school before so the staff were convinced that they were coming because they were dissatisfied. When the parents arrived they shook the teacher's hand and thanked her warmly. It turned out that their daughter was the first member of the family who had actually learnt to read well enough to understand the letters and leaflets that came into the house. The parents were proud and delighted as they were aware of, and accepted, their own difficulties and those of their children. Not only was the girl successful, but so were her parents who, despite their difficulties, were both in employment, kept and orderly home and sent polite, well-turned-out children into school every day.

It is sad that some people can only enjoy the feeling of success after they leave school. For them their experience of school can be a betrayal of their right to self-esteem throughout childhood and adolescence. The support staff at the student's side in the classroom is in a privileged position of being able to detect any small step towards understanding and to reinforce this. This should be pointed out to others so that they too can celebrate the success with the child. As advocates of the children they support they must constantly be alert to ways in which to build students' self-esteem.

Conclusion

Students with mild and moderate difficulties are a tremendously heterogeneous group, with a number of different causes for their difficulties. Whatever the cause of their difficulties, by the time they reach secondary school they will carry with them the history of many interactions and events in their lives. Some of these will have emotional and social consequences.

This group is extremely prone to being victims to bullies. This, and their frequent feeling of not being able to keep up with others often leads to depression in adolescence. This might present as lethargy so that they are blamed for laziness. Sensitive support staff can do a great deal to help these students at a crucial stage of their development.

Further reading

Barrett, H. and Jones, D. (1996) 'The inner life of children with moderate learning difficulties' in Varma, V. (ed.) *The Inner Life of Children With Special Needs*. London: Whurr.

Lorenz, S. (1998) *Children with Down's Syndrome: a guide for Teachers and Learning Support Assistants in Mainstream Primary and Secondary Schools*. London: David Fulton Publishers.

Varma, V. (ed.) (1996) *The Inner Life of Children with Special Needs*. London: Whurr.

Wise, L. and Glass, C. (2000) *Working with Hannah: a special girl in mainstream school*. London: Routledge Falmer. (An experience of Down's syndrome in mainstream.)

CHAPTER 5

Supporting Students with Specific Learning Difficulties

Students with specific learning difficulties are those who are most likely to need specialised support in mainstream classrooms. Although it is important to look at their needs separately from those of the students described in the previous chapter, this does not mean that students with moderate learning difficulties might not also have similar specific learning difficulties. Students with specific learning difficulties are often, perhaps usually, referred to as being 'dyslexic'. In the Warnock Report (DES 1978) There is some doubt cast on the existence of a 'dyslexic syndrome', but there is recognition of a group of students whose difficulties in specific areas of the curriculum are greater than their general ability would lead one to expect.

> Although there are no universally agreed criteria for distinguishing those children with severe and long-term difficulties in reading, writing and spelling from others who may require remedial teaching in these areas, there are, nevertheless, students whose disabilities are marked but whose general ability is at least average, and for whom distinctive arrangements are necessary. (Warnock Report: 218, 11.48)

There is a lack of agreement on a term to describe students with these specific difficulties both nationally and internationally. However, there is no question about the existence of such students and the concern that they cause to teachers and their parents.

The British Dyslexia Association

The British Dyslexia Association has the highest profile of any organisation supporting the needs of pupils in mainstream schools. The concern of parents, whose children were not learning to read with conventional teaching, despite adequate intelligence, and freedom from physical and emotional defect, led to the setting up of voluntary dyslexia associations.

Eight associations were formed between 1965 and 1972. In 1972 the British Dyslexia Association was formed as a national coordinating organisation. Its aims are to promote understanding of the problem of dyslexia and to support research into all aspects of the problem. The membership includes parents, teachers, psychologists and anyone interested in the problem of dyslexia.

The BDA produces an annual handbook which is full of information about services available to dyslexic pupils and their parents in the private sector as well as the public sector. It also contains articles on current developments and individual cases. In addition, they produce publications which describe recent research, educational developments and individual case histories. Details are to be found in the Appendix.

Definitions and descriptions of specific learning difficulties

There have been innumerable attempts to define the causes of specific learning difficulties. Much work was done in trying to establish an organic reason for these difficulties, especially as they seemed to run in families. There are a number of theories about the way both hemispheres of the brain are connected and there is no shortage of literature which gives detailed explanations of brain function (Tansley and Pankhurst 1981).

A more recent development concentrates on irregularities in the eyesight of some children with 'dyslexic'-type difficulties. An American psychologist, Helen Irlen (1991), discovered that certain children were helped to learn to read, or to speed up their reading, by placing a carefully selected tinted overlay on the printed page. The tests to diagnose whether a tinted overlay will help a reading problem is done by teachers who have received special training as screeners. The students who benefit most are those who report that they see words jump about, wobble or go wavy when they look at a page of print. They are also the students who become noticeably fatigued when they have to read for a long time. Irlen described the distortion they experienced as the Scotopic Sensitivity Syndrome (SSS). If, after a period of use, this overlay is seen to assist the student's ability to read print, spectacles with specially designed lens to filter light could be made after consultation with a specialist.

Although there has been much scepticism about the efficacy of coloured filters, since Helen Irlen's evidence was anecdotal rather than being the result of, or part of, a rigorous research project, there have been a number of both lay and professional supporters who can describe instances where the filters have made a dramatic difference in reading ability. Research that was started by the Medical Research Council's Applied Psychology Unit in Cambridge has been continued by Arnold Wilkins, now at the University of Essex. The results of this research are used by the Institute of Optometrists in this country (Wilkins *et al.* 2000). There is also a company which will reproduce texts on coloured paper (see VIVID books in the Appendix).

Class teachers and support staff may well come across pupils who use tinted filters or lenses and who are convinced of their usefulness. There is a theory (Cardinal *et al.* 1993) that these can be used as a placebo, making students feel that their difficulties are being noted and acted upon. They are therefore, in theory, going to make more effort with their work to show that the filters are effective. After all, these students will have been the focus of attention from the specialist who has prescribed the filters, and will have had money spent on them by their parents. Also, the fact that the student is using an overlay or spectacles with coloured lenses demonstrates that his or her difficulty has been recognised in the public arena. Interestingly, in the last four years coloured spectacles have been available over the counter and have become a fashion item for some young people!

The use of filters is gradually being backed up by research as well as experience and they are becoming available to more children. They are available from a number of optometrists. A colorimeter is used for diagnosis.

Classroom difficulties

It is essential for support staff, working closely with individual students, and SENCOs, giving advice to subject teachers, to be aware of all the theories and developments in aiding students with specific learning difficulties. However, the fact remains that, in a secondary school, our task is to help the child access the curriculum shared by his peers in the best way possible. Although, ideally, every teacher should be a special needs teacher, the constraints of time and place sometimes make the extra work required too difficult.

The earlier difficulties are identified, the less difficulty the student is likely to encounter in secondary school. Unfortunately there are some students who are not identified until just prior to secondary school transfer, or even later. It is easy to dismiss a child with specific difficulties as being lazy and unmotivated. If they have been through primary school, experiencing difficulty in every subject, there will probably be a lack of confidence and motivation. In the most recent research Daniel admitted that he had caused real grief to all his teachers because he had never been able to produce the work. He could understand and talk about it but was unable to write even when copying from the board. He became the class clown.

Warren was the third of three brothers who had specific learning difficulties. His problems were identified at the same time as a lecturer at the local Further Education college identified his eldest brother as being dyslexic. The diagnosis made a great deal of difference to both boys. However, Warren had already lost a lot of ground and most of his confidence. Instead of becoming the class clown he was withdrawn and often complained of stomach pains on school days.

However, some students blossom at secondary school. One such student was Christopher. It was thought by his primary school teachers that he would never cope in the large secondary school to which he was going. Apparently he sat on his own at primary school so there was always room for someone to sit beside him and support him, and he was the only one who never had any of his work displayed. The other children did not want him in their group when they were doing a project. I was expecting to meet a very depressed boy.

Two days after his arrival at secondary school some of his teachers asked why such a bright boy was in the lowest band. None of the newcomers had yet had to hand in any written work, but there had been plenty of opportunities to answer questions in class, and to join in with discussions. Christopher had a good vocabulary and general knowledge and at long last had the chance to shine at school. He had tended to be a 'wanderer' at primary school, so he had responded well to having to walk quite a long way between each lesson. By the time he had to present some written work he had gained confidence in his abilities and was motivated to ask for help at home and at school. He still has some problems, but no longer sees himself as one big problem.

The unfortunate situation arises with students who have literacy difficulties in primary school, that they may find themselves having to do even more reading and writing while their peers are doing more interesting tasks. It is also a problem that some children who receive an early diagnosis of dyslexia see themselves in a totally negative light. One boy was convinced that he could only make progress with a 'proper dyslexia teacher'(i.e. trained by the British Dyslexia Association). A parent was concerned that reading help with any other teacher for her son would mess up the work of 'his proper dyslexia teacher'. Both boys saw themselves as total problems who could only be helped by certain people. There is no doubt that people specifically trained to support a student with dyslexia can make a difference. However, staff with a knowledge of specific learning difficulties can help with strategies and reinforcing prior learning. Neither boy was able to see that there were many, many things he could do as well, if not better, than other children. Most teachers with a SEN qualification have done considerable work on dyslexia and are able to identify the specific needs of a student.

Structured Multi-sensory Literacy Programmes

If the student has a statement to support their need for help because of specific learning difficulties, it will nearly always specify that they should have a Multi-sensory Literacy Programme. There are a number of programmes available which have been prepared by professionals who have spent many years of their careers working out the best ways to help these students to learn to read, spell and write. One of the most popular is the *Alpha to Omega* programme (published privately in 1974 and now in its fourth edition published by Heinemann), which was devised by Professor Beve Hornsby, who founded the Hornsby International Centre which now trains teachers on both part-time courses and by distance learning. (Information about the Centre is given in the Appendix.)

If parents pay for individual tuition for a child with specific learning difficulties, especially if they employ a tutor recommended by the British Dyslexia Association, their child will almost certainly be taught using these materials and these methods in a very structured way. There are many dyslexia tutors who have not received a full teacher training but are specially trained to teach by this method. Children in primary schools who receive support from learning support teams, or from the school's own support teachers, may well benefit from these multi-sensory programmes of work.

A number of high schools are offering short sessions, using these programmes, for a few students, before and after school. An increasing number of schools in 2000 spoke of budgeting for dyslexia support. Because this support is given in small groups students have, unfortunately, to be withdrawn from the regular timetable. The two SENCOs who did this stressed how important it was not always to withdraw from the same lesson, and not to withdraw from Art, IT or PE. In fact these extra sessions are often during registration, and in the students' and the teachers' own time. This work is therefore dependent on the goodwill of the teacher and the motivation of the students. It is not easy to provide this kind of support in a secondary school. It is unfortunate that some students, like the two boys described at the end of the previous section, start secondary school believing that this is the only approach to literacy that will help them. The problem with using a multi-sensory programme is that it is best done individually, or in a small group. Unless this is offered before school begins it will entail withdrawal. Obviously as soon as you begin to withdraw a student from a secondary school classroom, you risk creating problems rather than solving them. However, schools that absolutely refused to consider withdrawing in 1993, are now using it in certain cases where all else has failed.

The multi-sensory approach is to learn by seeing, hearing, touching and moving. Support staff can often create the conditions to approach a science or French text in this way if they carefully keep students 'on task', listening to the teacher and following each word with a finger or a guide. Students with specific learning difficulties often need help to establish the habit of paying careful attention to the lesson. It is in this way that support staff can often be used quite intensively during the first few weeks at secondary school. Once a child gains confidence and experiences some success they will be more motivated to take control of their own learning. One of the advantages of working with secondary students in a multi-sensory way is that you can discuss with them what you are doing and why, and encourage them to think of strategies themselves.

Strategies for reading difficulties

Since it is not possible to work in a multi-sensory way with all students with specific learning difficulties, I am going to describe ways in which students have been helped in the classroom. There are many teachers who do not see themselves as experts in any kind of special educational need, who have devised effective, common-sense methods to help most of the students in their classes to learn. It is important that teachers share with each other any successful strategies they have.

If you know the student has difficulty with reading, and they have to read something on their own, it is a good idea to read the first paragraph with them while they look at the text. From the first paragraph it is usually possible to learn what the whole piece is going to be about. It also establishes the style of writing, such as whether it is humorous or serious, or if there are words in dialect which might alter the spelling of certain words. If pupils are in a situation where they are choosing their own books to read, there is a simple test which can be used to make sure the pupils do not choose books with too many words with which they will have difficulty (otherwise more than half of the lesson can be spent going up to ask for words or changing book after book). In the 'finger test' the student takes a book from the shelf. He opens it at the middle page and begins to read from the top. He places his little finger on the first word he cannot read. He places the ring finger on the next failed word, the middle finger on the next, and so on until the fingers and thumb of one hand are used. If he runs out of fingers before the end of the page, that book is too difficult for the time being. Students with specific learning difficulties are such fragile readers it is important that they are not put off trying to read books that present too much difficulty.

If a book has to be read because it is a set text, it could be made available on tape. Many books have been taped excellently by established actors. From time to time the abridged texts and tapes of classic novels are available cheaply from newsagents. These are worth collecting as a resource since they come with a booklet which gives background information of the story. Students who have listened to these texts often subsequently derive real pleasure from reading the book because they remember the story. Talking books for the visually impaired can also be a good source of reading materials for examination candidates with reading difficulties.

Sometimes members of a drama group welcome the opportunity to read texts on tape for a special needs department. This can mean having quite dramatic renderings of the first year Science course to which pupils can have access when they have to do homework from the textbook. Pupils who need this kind of help can bring their own tapes into school and have what is needed recorded on to it. Sometimes sixth formers who are experiencing some difficulty with the greatly increased study demands can benefit from trying out for themselves some of the strategies used for children with reading difficulties.

There are times, of course, when you want to know that the student with reading difficulties is actually using the support time for learning to read correctly. There is a valuable suggestion for making sure this is done in a handbook for helping adolescent dyslexics (Stirling 1985). The student is told to use a quiz of a specified number of questions on what he or she has just read. When he or she has finished, the teacher takes a few minutes reading through the passage chosen and read by the student before being asked the questions. This way the pupil reads carefully because he or she realises that they must know the answers, but the pupil is not in the position where they risk failure by being asked questions that they cannot answer. This method has been suggested to parents who want to know how they can help their children who have passed the stage where listening to them reading each evening is no longer appropriate. A child can be encouraged to prepare a quiz for a parent on the science read for homework. The parent must be prepared to be undismayed if he or she fails on some questions.

It is also important that there is plenty of reading matter available, of the kind that motivates young people to read. Scornful though many adults are of the *Readers' Digest* the articles have the advantage of being short and are usually high in human interest. Reluctant readers can become engrossed in articles from this and it has been known to give them a starting point for their own writing. Computer magazines and teenage magazines also motivate reluctant readers. Students with specific reading difficulties will only improve their reading skills if they have plenty of practice. For that reason it is important not to be dismissive of any reading matter which lacks the beauty and endurance of the classics. If a student becomes so engrossed in an account of a football match, or his favourite rock band, that he cannot be distracted, he must be reading with understanding.

Some students' reading difficulties are so great that they might never read for pleasure but only ever use reading as a tool. There are few students who cannot look up the television programmes in the paper, or read a letter or report that concerns themselves (unless it has been written in deliberately obscure language).

Strategies for writing difficulties

The student with writing difficulties is often labelled careless or untidy, unless they also have significant difficulties in reading and spelling. Since writing is a more creative activity than reading or spelling it is also more complex. Not only are there a variety of different styles of writing for different occasions and different audiences, but there are also fairly rigid rules to be obeyed.

There are two aspects to supporting a student with writing problems. The first is to help the student make his or her work look pleasant and inviting to read. A student wrote excellent stories where he kept a number of characters acting in a breathtaking manner until the end of the story. The stories were so eccentrically spelt and written that they took a couple of hours to decode. Even Kieran, the author, became confused when trying to read them back. The solution was to record the story on tape as he thought about it, and then using a Walkman and a laptop computer, listen to a few words at a time and type them out. After this the spell-checker was used and he had the satisfaction of producing excellent creative work. For the GCSE examination he had a scribe to write some papers but for other papers he had to work hard with his penmanship.

When Kieran has to write notes in Science, History or Geography he dictates them to his teaching assistant. She writes them in pencil in a simple flowing style which he later writes over, reading the notes as he does so. This method has been used with a number of students in this school. Some of them have been so encouraged with the appearance of their finished work that they have weaned themselves off help and have adopted this style. Because of the way the letters are linked, this style of writing also serves to reinforce spelling rules.

The SENCO in a selective boys' school, where a number of boys arrived with writing difficulties, recommended that they started off by writing on alternate lines in their books. Not only does this immediately make the writing easier for the teacher to read but it gives the work a less cluttered appearance. Also, many students with spelling difficulties, as well as writing difficulties, write with minuscule letters that are barely visible to the human eye. By using alternate lines, they develop a larger style of writing. A further advantage is that a student reaches the end of the book earlier and, if an improvement has been made, the old book can sooner be discarded, and there is an incentive to make a fresh start in a new book. The boys decide for themselves when they are ready to use all the lines and they might do this in some subjects before others. It is important that secondary students with any specific kind of learning difficulty have some kind of control over the strategies they are using.

Sometimes it is not just the penmanship that is difficult for students. They also have difficulty in constructing sentences and paragraphs. It is important for them to realise that a series of short sentences is preferable to long complex ones. Support staff can help to check whether there is a verb in each sentence, and whether the addition of an adjective or an adverb would make the sentence more meaningful or interesting. They can also help with the understanding of paragraphs as a group of adjacent sentences because of their relationship with each other. Learning to plan an essay at an early stage in secondary school life is very important for these students if they are to receive a grade in English examinations that reflects their general ability.

The English GCSE examination is a great worry for those with reading or writing difficulties. The choice of essay titles is a very important one. Students with these difficulties should have help with being able to determine which title will put them at the least disadvantage. An essay where the beginning or end of the story is given is very difficult to do well in as the style and the story have been predetermined and might not be a style familiar to the pupil. An essay demanding description is also a risk for those who have difficulty with remembering and spelling varied vocabulary. Probably an essay which depends on providing opinions is the safest to attempt. Advice should be given on preparing by jotting down ideas and facts before starting the essay. From Year 7, any help given with drafting and redrafting will be an investment for the time of examinations.

A personal laptop computer can be a tremendous help if the student is supported in learning to use it when it is provided. However, there is a danger that too often students who know that this is a recommendation on their statement look forward to it in joyful anticipation because they believe it will solve all their difficulties. An example of this was Anna. Anna was a 14-year-old girl with not only really severe reading, writing and spelling difficulties but also extremely well-developed techniques for avoiding putting pen to paper. She was given a sophisticated word processor as part of sponsorship from a local firm and proudly carried her machine, the envy of all her classmates, to all her lessons.

Unfortunately, one of the problems with her writing was that she had never sorted out the difference between upper case and lower case letters, and so often the middle letters in her words were upper case since she scattered capitals in a totally random fashion. Her inaugural session with the word processor could have provided the motivation for her to learn the function of upper case letters. However she just did everything completely in upper or lower case, depending on how the shift key was initially set. She also could have benefited from the built-in spell-checker but since she had never come across the word 'edit' (and to her 'consult dictionary', meant just that, and she had never found dictionaries much help) she soon lost enthusiasm for the machine. When the ink started to leak, she was told to take it to the office to be repaired. She did not collect it and I am sure she was left with an even greater sense of failure than before, because even with this miracle machine she had not produced good work.

In another school there is a policy of planning the introduction of the laptop computer to the child. The child is not lent a machine until there is someone in the room, such as support staff or a sixth former, who has time to supervise the student through the first couple of pieces of work and explain how the spell-checker works. At first the computer is lent on a trial basis, and its use is carefully evaluated by both student and teacher. Because of the difficulty of carrying extra equipment round the school, the smallest laptops possible which have full sized keyboards are used and there is access to a shared printer. If the introduction goes well and the student is benefiting from the use of the computer one will be allocated, and sometimes even a portable printer that can be taken home for homework is provided.

A laptop is only of value to a student with writing difficulties if functions such as 'cut' and 'paste', 'edit' and 'move file' are understood. Many students with specific learning difficulties have already suffered years of frustration, and it is important that what is meant to help them does not leave them with another experience of failure.

During the time between the two research projects far more students have a computer in their own home that belongs to them personally, or their family. Most have little difficulty in using any that might be provided by the school. However, it is important that there is an induction period since it cannot be assumed that all students have access to an up-to-date computer at home. Some home computers are used mainly as games machines and for access to the Internet, rather than to do extended pieces of writing.

Strategies for spelling difficulties

Words to help with spelling should be immediately entered into a little book which is easy to refer to. Often the support staff need to enter the word while the student is writing it into his classwork. At the beginning of the lesson, while the class is settling down, it can be useful to review what has been done in the student's books since your last support with him, and comment on any spelling error as you put the correct version in his book. It has to be their decision whether they change the spelling in the work already done, but if their specific learning difficulties are the reason for which they have been allocated support, I would not see this as cheating in any way.

It can be helpful, when students ask for a word, to say it a few times both as it is spelt and with the correct pronunciation. Students can often spell words that they have learned to mispronounce, especially those with a 'gh' in the middle. Because so many students make mistakes by missing out syllables, it is important to read back the work.

There are some students who are sufficiently motivated to use a commercially produced spell-checker very effectively. Spell-checkers have improved greatly and can recognise some of the more bizarre spellings such as 'nolij' for 'knowledge', 'creecher' for 'creature' and 'shofer' for 'chauffeur'. Those who have laptop computers usually have software with a spell-checker, but again they must have the motivation and understanding to use this. There is also a Spelling Checklist/Dictionary for Dyslexics (Stirling 1985) which is very useful and easy to use in the classroom.

It is difficult to teach spelling while supporting in a Science or Geography lesson but, in common with most support, it is often a matter of trying to increase an adolescent's confidence in his or her own ability to find the resources to help themselves. Frequently, rather than spelling the word that is requested, it is better to ask the student what they think the first letter will be? what is the sound it is linked to? are there other sounds before the end? and how does it end? At each stage prompting can help the child to discover not only the spelling but the rule, or the exception, as the case may be. One of the very satisfying aspects of supporting specific learning difficulties in secondary school classrooms is that the students are old enough to discuss the strategies they are using to overcome their difficulties, and sometimes they can be the ones who make the suggestions. The skill of the support staff is in motivating the students to want to develop the means to take control of their own learning. The role of the support staff is to mediate the learning and boost the student's confidence in their ability to manage their own problems.

Strategies for improving memory

Both short-term and long-term memory is seen as a vital element in specific learning difficulties. There is a theory (Morrison *et al.* 1977) that 'dyslexics' hold images in the mind for a shorter time than students without these difficulties. Farnham-Diggory(1978) suggests that the act of remembering is not a passive one, and it is necessary to have programmes for remembering that involve, 'attention, rehearsal and other kinds of information management'. The classic way of teaching dyslexic pupils, and indeed other students also, to learn spellings is to instruct them to: look, cover, try, look; and if you do not succeed do this again. This method is also used to learn mathematical formulae and facts from other subjects and also modern language vocabulary.

The multi-sensory programmes that were mentioned earlier all take into account memory difficulties. A favourite maxim of the British Dyslexia Society is: If I hear, I forget; If I see, I remember; If I touch, I understand.

Some students with specific learning difficulties find that they remember best if they repeat things over and over again to themselves as soon as they have been told. An example of this is the young man who repeated his homework over and over to himself because his writing was so bad he knew neither he or his mother would be able to read it when he arrived home. When, at the age of 14, he started to learn to skate, he amazed his coaches by remembering everything he had been taught from lesson to lesson. Immediately after each lesson he would do two or three total reruns of it on ice, repeating everything the teacher had said. He often ran through the dialogue again in the car on the way home. He did not leave the ice until he was happy that he had internalised the lesson. Within five years he was in the British Olympic Ice Dance Squad, where he used the same method to memorise complicated steps and patterns of all the international compulsory ice dances. He is now an accomplished show skater. People often remark how well he would have done if he had started at an earlier age. I doubt he would have achieved anywhere near his present success as he did not have the confidence in his ability early on to take charge of his own learning.

Some students with a memory problem feel there is nothing they can do about it. However, it is possible to devise discreet methods of prompting the memory. I am sorry that some teachers seem constrained to punish students who use the back of their hand as an impromptu notebook (there is no danger unless there is an open wound or if Indian ink is used). A cluster of single letters can contain a myriad of reminders, as students can be helped to work out their own code of abbreviations to trigger recall. A pad of really tiny 'stick its' kept in a purse or a pocket can be useful for small notes, and reminders can be stuck on books, etc. There are also small, inexpensive recording machines available that will hold about five minutes worth of recorded messages and fit in a blazer pocket. For students who have mobile phones by which they can send e-mails, e-mailing themselves about homework and equipment to remember is a possibility.

Strategies for improving organisational skills

Thinking skills were mentioned in the previous chapter on moderate learning difficulties. A methodical course on thinking skills would certainly benefit most dyslexic students. In the early 1990s there were a number of local groups where psychologists and teachers met to discuss the role of thinking skills in the curriculum. A large firm in Kent sponsored such a group which met in their conference suite. All young people joining the firm did a course of thinking skills as part of their induction. The method used was Instruments Enrichment (IE) devised by the Israeli psychologist, Reuven Feuerstein. A document on the Key Stage 3 curriculum, issued by the DfEE in April 2001 advocates 'Piloting approaches to the teaching of thinking skills to enable pupils to analyse and use knowledge more effectively, to solve problems individually and to think creatively.'

The value of thinking skills is that it encourages students to think about their own methods of thinking (meta-cognition) and by doing this to be able to exercise more control over the efficiency of their thinking. Children with specific learning difficulties are rarely able to succeed when they attack a task in an impulsive or random way. The thinking skills movement was inspired by those who saw a need to prevent children, especially those who had had an unsettled early life, from doing everything in a totally haphazard and unplanned way. It was to help them to internalise a sense of order and purpose in tasks. Most programmes that succeed with dyslexics contain these elements.

Support staff in the classroom, especially in the earlier years of secondary education, need to help their protégées with developing a ritual for setting out their work neatly. Help given early on can increase confidence as the work is satisfying to look at. This is an area where support staff really need to consult the class teacher to find out what will be required throughout the year. It is, of course, easier in a school where all the children carry a small book, known as a diary or a journal, where they note down their homework, teachers write messages home, and parents sign it at regular intervals, acknowledging they have seen it. If there is a policy about how the date is written, widths of margins and the format of headings, etc., it is worth clipping a model headed page into the diary that the student carries, so that they can refer to it before putting pen to paper.

The diary or journal will be the lifeline between the student with SpLD, the school and the parents. The support staff can use the time before and after the lesson making sure that the diary is up to date, that the student is using the right page and has not accidentally skipped a day, a week, a month or even a term. Some students consistently forget PE and technology equipment, and when you look in their diaries you find entries made at random. I liked the idea of one teacher who gave each student a rubber band to mark the page in the diary (placed over the pages between the back cover and the right page). Every Monday morning she checks that everyone is on the right page. Although there is a fair bit of twanging of rubber bands, it does help those who find self-organisation difficult.

With younger students, support staff can sometimes help by going through a student's school bag (in their presence, of course, and with their permission) and collecting equipment, notes, etc., that have gathered at the bottom. If it is a bag with a number of separate compartments the support staff can talk through with the student how he or she can set aside each area for a different purpose. If this is done in the first few weeks of the first year it can start a habit that will stand the student in good stead throughout their school life. A student who has poor organisational skills might well come from a home where a parent has similar difficulties (see Chapters 6 and 7 also). It is acknowledged that reading, writing and spelling difficulties can run in families but not so often suggested that memory and organisational difficulties might also.

Students with organisational difficulties will need a great deal of support early in their secondary school life, but this should not be support that takes over the responsibility for remembering. Any help given should be discussed and the student should be invited to suggest strategies that they might use to help themselves. Sometimes going round with a classmate who is well organised and knows the timetable and what is needed for each lesson can help greatly during the first half term, as long as the student with special needs does not become dependent, but uses this as a temporary crutch.

In the higher forms students with organisational difficulties will need extra support a few weeks before examinations and when assignments are due in. It will be important for them to compile a study plan and a time management plan. Although they might need considerable help initially this should gradually be weaned away, especially if the student is thinking of going on to further or higher education.

The importance of preserving self-esteem

It is unfortunate that, in order to obtain extra resources for support in school, the learning and ability deficits of the student have to be emphasised. The important fact about students with SpLD is that their learning difficulties are specific and not 'across the board', as are those of students with moderate learning difficulties. There are more things that these students can do than they cannot do. This is important because, from the start, they must learn to use those strengths to compensate and devise strategies for overcoming areas of difficulty.

For many parents it is a serious blow to find out that their children have serious learning difficulties. The children will have heard their parents expressing their concern and might pick up a certain hopelessness from them. This is confirmed when they know they have statements of special needs and even an extra person to support them in some lessons. It is important for their self-esteem that it is a partnership between the students and the support staff. When sitting with these students in the classroom it is important that support staff treat them as intelligent human beings with their own ability to reason; they might then feel confident enough to let others in the group work out strategies with them to overcome their difficulties.

I taught one adolescent who was convinced he would never be able to do anything because he was 'dyslexic'. His parents were very involved in the local dyslexia association and had tried to enlist as many experts as possible to help him. He had no confidence in his own ability to do anything. However, when he arrived in the Science lab of his new secondary school it was not immediately obvious to anyone that he had a problem since early lessons were oral and mainly about lab safety and how experiments should be done. He had plenty of common sense and was often ahead of the others in answering. When experiments were started, he was often the one with the best ideas on how a theory could be tested and validated. Unfortunately, it was not possible to read anything he had written down, if indeed he had written anything down. Often when told to write he would delay as long as possible and then stop when he reached the first word he was not sure about spelling. When I was supporting him he dictated his notes to me, I wrote them in pencil and he wrote over them. This way he gained confidence with writing and began to realise his ability to spell was improving. Fortunately, when the boys had to chose a partner with whom to work several offered to work with him because he had good ideas. He wisely chose a partner who was extremely neat and tidy, although lacking in flair and originality. They made a good partnership and Robert's self-esteem increased so much from being in this partnership, especially as he was able to help his partner as much as his partner helped him.

This kind of arrangement, which exploits the talents of all, can often happen in lessons such as Science, Technology, Geography and History, but is more difficult in Modern Languages. Although some students with specific learning difficulties have an excellent ear in oral work, most have difficulty with the reading, writing and spelling of a foreign language. French seems to cause more problems than German or Spanish because of the discrepancy (to English students) between how a word is written and how it is pronounced. It is important that teachers of Modern Languages are aware of the difficulties experienced by these students, so that they do not put too much emphasis on written work. It often helps to point out to students with difficulty that it is more likely that they will be called upon to speak or listen to a foreign language, than that they will have to read or write it. Fortunately the National Curriculum puts as much emphasis on speaking and listening as on reading and writing.

It is of paramount importance that any support given is geared towards total independence and that students are always aware that it is their own strengths upon which they are building.

Choices after school

It is also important that the student with SpLD does not see the choice of an academic pathway after school as the only way to gain success. Although some students do gain A-level passes, A-level puts tremendous pressure on young people who have never had difficulties. Young people with SpLD will need consideable professional support in selecting the right pathway to follow after school.

For young people who have always had considerably more difficulty than their peers in reading and writing but have good cognitive and oral skills, the GNVQ (General National Vocational Qualifications) route could be very suitable. These courses are available in Colleges of Further Education and Sixth Forms. The emphasis is on the kind of thinking, recording, communication and reference to sources that would be required in the workplace. At higher levels these courses are demanding of time and planning, and have the rigour of A-level courses without the demand for such a high level of literacy. There is also a requirement to be able to function as a member of a team with a specific task to do, within a certain time. These courses are not an easy option, and employers are aware of what each level of achievement means. At higher levels they are an alternative entry requirement for university.

Because of the rigour of these courses they are not suitable for all school leavers. Some will find NVQs (National Vocational Qualifications), the vocational qualifications that are based on the workplace, much more suitable. These qualifications validate practical competencies in a very systematic way.

It is important that whatever dyslexic school leavers do after school it is what they really want, and not undertaken just to satisfy what others think they should do. Because of their difficulties, these students have to be really motivated if their choices involve further study, since this will always entail more effort. The young man who skates hated Modern Languages at school but having spent two years training in Paris, and now skating in a show in Germany, he converses in both languages (although he can read little, and write less!). It is vital to focus on the young person's strengths when supporting them through the transition from school to further education or work.

Further reading

Miles, T. (1996) 'The inner life of the dyslexic child' in Varma, V. (ed.) *The Inner Life of Chldren with Special Needs*. London: Whurr.

Miles, T. R. and Miles, E. (1999) *Dyslexia: A Hundred Years On*, 2nd edn. Buckingham: Open University Press.

Montgomery, D. (1997) *Spelling: Remedial Strategies*. London: Cassell.

Montgomery, D. (1998) *Reversing Lower Attainment*. London: David Fulton Publishers.

Peer, L. and Reid, G. (eds) (2001) *Dyslexia - Successful Inclusion in Secondary Schools*. London: David Fulton Publishers.

Pollock, J. and Waller, E. (1997) *Day to Day Dyslexia in the Classroom*. London: Routledge.

Ripley, K., Daines, B. and Barrett, J. (1997) *Dyspraxia: A Guide for Teachers and Parents*. London: David Fulton Publishers.

CHAPTER 6

Supporting and Understanding the Disruptive Student in the Classroom

In the first edition of this book this chapter was entitled, 'The Impossible Child', but publications since have added to our knowledge of suitable interventions for the children who make life in the classroom such a challenge for the teacher (Rodgers 2000, Cooper and O'Regan 2001). Teachers with whom I spoke during my most recent research indicated that students with emotional and behavioural difficulties are those with whom they need the most help. In rewriting this book I had decided to split my previous chapter on emotional and behavioural difficulties into two parts: concerning those conditions with a label and those conditions without a label. However, speaking to many teachers about their work, it is clear that in the classroom the highest priority is how to teach the student effectively in a classroom setting, regardless of the nature of his or her difficulty.

There are a group of students with emotional and behavioural difficulties for whom there are other problems. These are often the invisible students; the ones who, in a busy classroom, often make little impact but whose needs are every bit as great as those whose presence we cannot ignore. Whatever the reason for their withdrawal from those round them they frequently underachieve, and have their own very special needs. Again, some might have a label, and others not, but the strategies for facilitating their learning are more important than the reason for their failure to engage fully with the life of the classroom. They will be the subject of Chapter 7.

> 'That boy has got problems with his reading, his comprehension, in getting things together enough to get them down on paper ... This boy not only needs learning support, he needs one-to-one to keep him at it. He takes advantage. It's not just learning support, it's behavioural support. Really I am not sure that dire cases like this should be in mainstream.'

This boy is fairly typical of the students who are often allocated support in the mainstream school, and the student in question could well be a girl. It is their tendency to disrupt the class and affect the quality of teaching that causes as much concern as their learning difficulty. It is also a common complaint that such students need constant attention in 'getting things together' and 'keeping at it'. They also usually have well-honed avoidance techniques, which can impede the work of all the pupils in the class.

The under-extended able child

Sometimes bad behaviour might be the reaction of the student who is being under-extended and no longer finds any challenge in the classroom. Unfortunately students, especially boys, have quite cruel names for those of their number who excel and request more challenging work. The very able child, if frustrated by work that makes too few demands, sometimes becomes the class-clown during the lesson and yet still hands in well-executed homework, despite giving the appearance of not having paid attention during the lesson. The SENCO in a selective school commented, 'There are a few very clever boys who are failed by the curriculum. There are a few boys at the upper end of the school who channel their high ability into getting into trouble, lots of trouble. When they decide to do something really wrong it is really quite a trouble to us because they have the intelligence to really annoy us.'

Could it be Attention Deficit Disorder?

The child who is described as impossible by teachers is the one that crosses the limits which few students dare to challenge. Very often when teachers express concern about the effect of these students on their teaching and on the learning of the rest of their class, they are asked to review their own teaching skills. It is often only when the student finally takes on a member of the senior management team that meetings are held, and there is concern that the student should either be brought under control or excluded.

Very often the school already has a well-considered whole-school policy for dealing with behaviour. Sometimes this includes a reward system or a system of yellow and red cards, familiar in the context of soccer matches. These devices can sometimes be effective in curbing the behaviour of students before they disrupt the education of other students too severely.

Nevertheless most teachers will have heard more and more of a condition known as Attention Deficit Disorder (ADD). There are two subtypes of this disorder. It can present with hyperactivity (AD/HD) or it can present without activity. The subtype with hyperactivity will be described in this chapter. The main symptoms for this disorder are: hyperactivity, impulsiveness, and difficulty in paying attention. There are often difficulties in short-term memory. Because this chapter is about students with emotional and behavioural difficulties which present as acting out behaviour AD/HD will be described, but it is important to bear in mind that not every student who presents with these behaviours has AD/HD.

The criteria for AD/HD have been identified and entered into the American Diagnostic Symptoms Manual. Among these are behaviours which are quite normal for a number of children, especially young children. It is important that at least nine of these symptoms are present, with some intensity, and before the age of seven, for AD/HD to be considered. *A diagnosis of AD/HD can only be made by a paediatrician,* after collecting evidence from the school, the parents or whoever cared for the student in infancy and preferably, his or her peers. However, these are the criteria:

- often fidgets with hands or feet or squirms in seat;
- has difficulty in remaining seated when told to do so;
- is easily distracted by external stimuli;
- has difficulty awaiting turns in group situations;
- often blurts out answers before they have been completed;
- has difficulty in following through instructions from others (not due to oppositional behaviour or failure of comprehension);
- has difficulty is sustaining attention in tasks and play activities;
- often shifts from one uncompleted activity to another;
- has difficulty playing quietly;
- often talks excessively;
- often interrupts or intrudes on others, e.g. butts into other children's games;
- often does not seem to listen to what is being said to him or her;
- often loses things necessary for tasks and activities at school or at home;
- often engages in physically dangerous activities without considering the possible consequences (not for the purpose of thrill seeking).

It is only AD/HD or ADD if at least nine of these criteria apply.

What if it seems to be AD/HD?

AD/HD is the most controversial concept for schools since the original identification of dyslexia, or specific learning difficulties. In an era and climate which encourages us to look to differentiation within the curriculum to solve students' special needs, we are being told that there are indeed special needs that are within the child. AD/HD has probably caused the fiercest controversy because from the beginning it has been inextricably linked with the taking of a Class A drug, Ritalin. There are other psycho-stimulants also used but this is the most common. The prospect of using a psycho-stimulant drug to change a student's behaviour is unacceptable to a number of teachers, as it is to many parents of students. Indeed many students are contained in schools with the intervention of behavioural programmes that are backed up by parents at home.

However, this is a distressing disorder for students who genuinely wish to do their work and please their parents and teachers, but find themselves constantly in trouble at home and school for behaviour that really is beyond their control. Often by the time they reach the secondary school, if they have not already been diagnosed and treated, they are already showing signs of oppositional behaviour and conduct disorder. The medication for these students helps them to focus on the task in hand and to control their constant impulses. It is interesting that a psychologist in 1890 wrote:

> There is a normal type of character, for example, in which impulses seem to discharge so promptly into movements that inhibitions get no time to arise. These are the 'dare devil' and 'mercurial' temperaments, overflowing with animation and fizzling with talk … (William James (1890) in *Principles of Psychology*)

It is interesting that we often describe these children with 'mercurial' temperaments as being 'like quicksilver' in their response to some situations. It is indeed often difficult, and a very subjective decision, to determine when behaviour ceases to be within a normal range and requires intervention.

In the last few years schools have often not known that a student has AD/HD until a packet of Ritalin is left in the school office for administration at lunch-time. The NICE (National Institute for Clinical Excellence) issued guidelines for the prescription of Ritalin in November 2000. These guidelines state that Ritalin should not be prescribed without some input from the school about the student's behaviour. There is an instrument below which I have adapted from an original one by Sam Goldstein, an American expert on the subject (Goldstein and Goldstein 1995). It can easily be used by a second person in the classroom, such as support staff.

This instrument looks at four common behaviours of students with AD/HD: talking out of turn, out of seat behaviour, attention-seeking or not paying attention, and disruptive behaviour. The method is to have a sheet of paper as shown in Figure 6.1, with boxes for ticking the various behaviours.

The observer does this at regular intervals. I find 30 seconds a good interval. As well as looking at the behaviour of the student giving cause for concern, it is useful to have a 'control' child who is within the field of vision of the observer. One would expect the observed child to have far more ticks than the control. If this is not the case it might be that the control is noisier because his voice has broken first, or he might seem to be all over the place because he is bigger than the others, or distinctive in some way such as hair or skin colour, and therefore has a higher profile when the noise rises and teaching becomes more difficult.

The test should be performed three times in different situations since each different lesson puts different demands on the student who has difficulty with behaviour and organisation. If the result is a forest of ticks then the class teacher or the teaching assistant can sit down quietly with the subject and discuss the result and what needs to be done to decrease the unwanted behaviours.

The student is then told that the test will be done again in three to six weeks time in order to help him or her to develop more acceptable behaviour. The next time the support does the test the subject will know it is being done and one would expect an almost clear sheet. If this is not so there is some evidence that the student has difficulty is controlling their own impulses. The process is repeated again after three to six weeks and if the result is still bad it is time to suggest to the student that perhaps they need more help and this should be discussed further with parents and the school psychologist as you know that the student is trying to improve but has real difficulty doing so.

This test is equally useful for a student who does not have AD/HD but has fallen into the habit of these behaviours. It gives a non-threatening reason for discussing behaviour and rewarding improvement. It is also useful to have this test at hand when parents of difficult students arrive at school, waving the latest article about AD/HD from a popular magazine or paper and 'want the school's support' for a diagnosis. This is particularly the case now that a Disabled Living Allowance is granted to some parents of children with AD/HD. The completed TOAD test is documentary evidence that you have taken the parent seriously. It can also be used as assessment for Stage 2 of the Code of Practice.

Name:				Control:			
Talking	Out of seat	Attention	Disruption	Talking	Out of seat	Attention	Disruption
/ / / /	/ / /	/ /		/			
/ /		/	/				
		/			/	/	
/ /	/	/	/ /	/			
/	/ /						
/ / /			/				
	/ /						
/		/	/	/ /			

Figure 6.1   TOAD test (Talking, Out of seat, Attention, Disruption)

If AD/HD is diagnosed

If AD/HD is diagnosed the school should have had input before the decision was taken. Whether the option of medication is taken up is the decision of the parent, sometimes in conjunction with the child. Many parents are reluctant for their child to be medicated. NICE see medication as being used in conjunction with behaviour programmes and input from the psychologist. Certainly medication alone will not solve the student's problems, but it can make it easier to devise strategies to help the child right away. There are a number of strategies that can be used in the classroom. Most involve constant monitoring and encouragement by the teacher or teaching assistant. This is a situation where support staff, who are aware of how a student with AD/HD feels in school, can make an enormous difference to the student's learning. Children with AD/HD, when they come to school, feel:

- worried that they might not be able to follow instructions;
- scared about not being able to get all their work finished;
- embarrassed that their work does not look as nice or is not 'as good as' most other students' work;
- concerned that they could not or did not write the ideas in their head;
- frustrated that they are unable to control their behaviour or moods;
- afraid that other students will be annoyed with them;
- anxious about loosing track, daydreaming, checking out and needing to move around.

The support staff who understand these fears can be there to talk them through some difficult situations and help them to slow down enough to understand tasks before they start.

Much has been said about where these students should sit in the classroom. It is necessary to understand that they have such high alertness that, if there is anything going on inside or just outside the classroom, that might take precedence over what the teacher is trying to teach. Therefore although the front row is always recommended, too near to the door, or an open window is not. They work best in a classroom where informal talking is kept to the very minimum. Other students will often goad them in order to experience an impulsive outburst. Support in the classroom includes being very aware of any undercurrent of provocation.

Just in the manner suggested for dyslexic students, these students complete work best when it is reduced to manageable parts and they can complete one section before proceeding to the next. They need frequent, sincere feed back. They also genuinely need, at times, to be able to walk about. Perhaps between tasks in a long lesson they can go to the library for a book or to the cupboard for other equipment. Sometimes, especially if the morning dose of Ritalin is wearing off, it is necessary to offer the opportunity for a walk, even if support staff have to accompany the student.

With students on medication there can be a kick-back effect at the end of the morning, especially if it is a very long morning. Often it is the staff at school who are most aware of the effect of the medication on the child. The TA can be alert to this. The school should always be consulted about an effective level of medication.

One student whom I supported had half his second dose during the second break of a morning that started at 8.45 a.m. and ended at 1.15 p.m. Ritalin is in the system for only four to five hours. Taking 5mg at the end of the ten minute break at midday meant that Ben could then go through until after lunch before having the rest of the 15mg dose. He had trouble with managing to do his homework and, when he went into Year 9, a decision was made for him to have a 5mg dose after school. Not only did this help him to sustain effort to complete his homework, but he also slept better.

I stress the giving of the drug after lunch although many schools have students lined up for their pill as soon as morning school ends. Unfortunately this medication makes some children nauseous when they take it, and being an amphetamine it is an appetite suppressant. The student who is given his first dose before breakfast and his second before lunch may feel hungry and bad-tempered for most of the day. It was thought to stunt the growth of small children but this is probably because they were having it before meals. If the office staff cannot fit in with this regime perhaps support staff can make themselves available to administer the medication at a suitable time. In some schools students look after their own pills. This is thought to recognise their responsibility and maturity. It also leaves them open to the blandishments of those who are already misusing and dealing Ritalin on the streets. Professionals in the drug misuse field are concerned that quantities of Ritalin are falling into the wrong hands.

Pseudo AD/HD

This is an expression coined by Professor Paul Cooper in his book *AD/HD in the Classroom* (1996). It refers to the condition of those who might seem to have nine or more of the symptoms and yet do not have AD/HD. These symptoms may be caused by a number of other things, including bereavement or other traumatic events. However, they will not have been evident before the age of seven, not have always had such an impact on the life of the sufferer. Parents or teachers who expect too much and exert too much pressure on young people can cause this. A young person growing up in an environment where adults are violent, abusive and impulsive might see this behaviour as normal. Pseudo AD/HD is normally not experienced for so long, or at such a great intensity, nor does it have such a damaging social effect.

This is sometimes a problem to ascertain. Since AD/HD is believed to be 60 per cent genetic (Cooper and O'Regan 2001), it is impossible to rule out the possibility of AD/HD because the child's home seems chaotic. It could well be chaotic because one or both of the parents have AD/HD. Sometimes parents are diagnosed at the same time as their children and the medication helps them to change to a more organised lifestyle.

There are other chromosomal conditions where the behaviour is similar to that of students with AD/HD, and the same strategies can be very effective.

William's syndrome

This is a little-known syndrome that affects children's ability to learn. Although it is evident from babyhood, and can be diagnosed by a blood test, it is so rare that some doctors might never encounter a case. It is a genetic condition caused by a missing chromosome and is thought to affect 1:10,000 children (ADD & AD/HD=1:20).Children with William's lack concentration, they have no analytical skills, and have difficulty reading and writing. They would rather talk to the teacher than concentrate. Often their incessant chatter is to hide their nervousness. In the classroom they present as hyperactive and have great difficulties in making friends with their peers, as do those with AD/HD. They have little coordination because the physical condition they have involves a lack of flexibility in their muscles and ligaments. For this reason they are always wanting to go to the lavatory. Because of poor coordination, their ability to play games and do PE deteriorates with age, leading to teasing from other students. Because of the inflexibility they all have very similar appearance with elfin-like features, weak eyes and muscles, stunted growth, dislike of loud noise. They have an almost telepathic empathy and a need for constant communication. They have wide upturned mouths which seem to be always smiling and turned up noses. It is therefore important for teachers not to confuse their fixed expression with insolence when they are being reprimanded.

Because of their low academic ability they are often not in mainstream. If they are there they will need both learning and behavioural support. There is a William's Trust which produces information and a video for teachers. Most children with William's will have been diagnosed before they reach secondary school. However, I have recently heard of undiagnosed William's' students in an FE college.

Asperger syndrome and AD/HD

It is not unusual for students with Asperger syndrome also to be diagnosed with ADD and AD/HD. In the case of Asperger's with AD/HD, both disorders involve sensory integration problems. This means that the student tends to be overstimulated by changes, and by incoming visual, auditory and tactile information. It is important that support staff are aware of this, as, for example, a gentle hand on the arm to urge a student along the corridor can be interpreted as a push. The normal buzz of the classroom can seem like a mighty roar if the student has the two disorders. Added to these problems, the student is prone to erupt into explosive anger at small provocation.

I have deliberately referred to Asperger's, rather than autism in general because this covers such a range of ability and behaviour, whereas students with Asperger syndrome are usually believed to have greater insight into their own behaviour. However, students with autism also have similar, in fact more intense, sensitivities which mean they are prone to, what appear to others, to be irrational rages. Support staff need to be alert to the triggers for these explosions and try to divert them. Sometimes when moving around the school it is a matter of the support staff protecting a zone around the student and making sure he or she is not pushed or touched. The student should not be in a position where they do not know where they are going and needs to be close to the crowd to be sure of reaching their destination. If there is to be a change of room it is important to explain this to the student as soon as possible, and then again just before it happens, if possible explaining why it is necessary.

AD/HD and Asperger's both involve different social difficulties. The student with Asperger's, or indeed autism, is unable to consider or empathise with his or her peers, whereas the student with AD/HD is often rejected by peers because of his of her behaviour. Because challenging behaviour from these students is usually triggered by frustration or fear, understanding support is the key to their continued presence in mainstream. More about these students will be provided in Chapter 7.

Gilles de Tourette's syndrome

Because the early onset of this disorder is very similar to AD/HD there was a fear that medication for AD/HD might be triggering the disorder. However, there is a very strong genetic indication and young people who develop this disorder usually have an older relative who has been a sufferer. The disorder is an inherited neurological one, characterised by repeated involuntary movements and uncontrollable vocal sounds called tics. In a few cases such tics can include inappropriate words and phrases.

I quote here a poem written by a 17-year-old sufferer of the syndrome.

> Maybe I spit, maybe I swear
> or constantly tap my hand
> How do I explain these things to you
> when I myself don't understand?
> Yes, it hurts me deep inside
> When I hear the taunting words you say.
> Jason Valencia, in Shimberg (1995)

The symptoms of Tourette's generally appear before the individual is 18 years old. Although TS symptoms range from mild to quite severe, the majority of cases fall into the mild category. The first symptoms of TS are usually facial tics – commonly eye-blinking. With time, other motor tics may appear, such as head jerking, neck stretching, foot stamping, or body twisting and bending.

Often a young person with Tourette's will continuously clear their throat, sniff, grunt, yelp, bark or shout. Another symptom is touching people excessively or repeating actions obsessively and unnecessarily. Although these are described as 'involuntary' actions, the impulse is very, very strong. There are people with Tourette's who can suppress the tics for hours at a time, only to have an excessively strong outburst as soon as the control is relaxed. The presence of a young person with Tourette's in the classroom obviously puts extra strain on the teacher, but effort has to be made to work with the other students so that they accept the behaviours that cannot be changed. The more stress the student is under to suppress the tics, the more difficult it is to do so.

Sometimes, with enormous effort, a student will manage to suppress the tics during a lesson in which there has been an important visitor, or a vital test, only to be told in the next lesson that if they can do this for an hour, why not all day. Tics worsen in stressful situations and improve when the student relaxes and becomes fully absorbed in an activity. This is where support staff can help to make sure that stress is kept to a minimum and that activities which fully involve the student are undertaken.

A few students with TS will engage in self-harming behaviours, such as lip and cheek biting and head banging. There are also a few who suffer from copralalia (constantly repeating phrases and words). Occasionally this might be a swear word or a racial epithet. It is thought that it is sometimes the 'forbiddenness' of the words that impels the person with TS to say what would normally be against their will.

Both Attention Deficit Disorder and Tourette's syndrome are believed to be caused by an abnormal metabolism dopamine and serotonin in the neurotransmitters. Much research is being done and there are extensive web sites devoted to Autism (including Asperger syndrome), ADD and Tourette's syndrome.

The interface between learning difficulties and behaviour

In the previous chapter on Specific Learning Difficulties (SpLD) the link was made between constant academic failure and avoidance and diversionary techniques in the classroom. What starts as breaking a pencil, just so that work can be delayed by having to go to the front to use a pencil sharpener, can develop into creating disruptive incidents. Three different boys with SpLD and two girls explained how their challenging behaviour had started from pure frustration at being faced with work they could not do. This had progressed to major incidents where either the student was sent from the classroom or as one of the boys said,

> 'Suddenly I find I have gone right over the top. I know I have lost it and I am going to hit someone unless I get out so I just run.'

This boy had been excluded for running away from a teacher through a busy car park. The school felt they could no longer take the risk.

One of the girls explained that she had lost the confidence to attempt any work on her own so if support staff were not there she would shout at the teachers until they came to help her. She said,

> 'All the time I am worrying about getting more behind if I am not given help right away so if they don't come, I start swearing at them. Then I know I have gone too far so I just lose it and run out.'

Another of the girls knew that she was powerful and strong and because she involved herself in physical fights others were afraid of her. She said,

> 'I go and sit near one of the boffs and threaten her if she won't help me. I don't want support staff helping me or else everyone thinks you are thick.'

The boy who described running out was also dyspraxic, but coped with PE by always playing the fool and distracting the others. He said he so enjoyed the laughter at first that he became addicted to it. He said sadly,

> 'The trouble is my mates like football. They get angry when they miss some of the lesson because the teacher won't start until everyone is ready to listen. He tries to help me play but I am hopeless so I tie my shoelaces together and pretend it is because I am thick.'

There is no doubt that these students place a huge burden on teachers. Unfortunately by the time they reach secondary school the failure and the attitudes to it are often very entrenched. Schools where investment was being made in regular classes for students with SpLD were making some headway but as a parent of a Year 9 boy said,

> 'He is now being withdrawn for an hour a week, instead of doing German [a second modern foreign language] but it isn't enough. Some of this time has to be spent reading the book the rest of the class are reading. I have put it on tape for him… took me three weekends. It is all in American slang… words he is never likely to use. That extra time should be spent teaching him to read and write English.'

Parents were very aware of the link between their children's behaviour and their learning difficulties. Many of them had pleaded for extra help throughout their junior school years but had felt they had been ignored. One school used the additional money they had for learning support in creating two classes of 12 for the 24 weakest students to come into the school. They had two support staff in these classes for nearly all lessons. Although it was a very expensive exercise the benefits of the first cohort were evident in Year 8 where the classes had been combined and had one teaching assistant. It was hoped that by the time this group reached Year 9 most would be confident readers and learners. This school held classes before and after school for students who still needed help but did not want their friends to know. The before school classes were very popular.

Conduct disorders

Although there is an official DSM (a condition included in the American Diagnostic Symptoms Manual) for Conduct Disorder, I use this term loosely to include those students who present problems throughout their school life. Many of these students could be said to have been socially excluded from an early age because of their life history. There are students from poor homes, on sink estates, with parents who are inadequate, who do, however, go on to thrive at school and regard school as a haven. However, there are probably more, especially since the influence of market forces in education, who are disaffected from an early age.

Intervention for these children can be successful if started at an early enough age. The widespread revival of the 'Nurture Groups', which were successful in the Inner London Education Authority (ILEA) identifies such children at reception class age and nurtures them for a year. The Pyramid Trust offers Year 3 screening to schools, followed by self-esteem building 'clubs' for those who are already falling behind, but by Year 7 it is often too late for these kinds of intervention to be successful. Some schools are finding that Circle Time for Year 7 students can help them to think through their behaviour, and the effect of that behaviour on others. Lucky Duck Publishing Company, run by George Robinson, the ex-head of a special school, and Barbara Maines, an educational psychologist, produces good packages for these students.

Many schools are now involving youth workers in school life since these professionals, who work in less formal ways, can often make a difference to self-concept and attitude to learning. The support staff who work with these students have to patiently try to form a supportive and trusting relationship, while treating the students as potential learners. The government initiative to train learning mentors for those who are showing signs of disaffection will place more support in the classroom. It is too early to evaluate the impact of the new government agency, Connexions, on the management of these students (see Chapter 10).

There are likely to be a number of agencies working with these young people, especially if they have been involved in the criminal justice system. It is important that there is communication between these professionals, although issues of confidentiality will be important. It is necessary that whoever works with these youngsters is able to give them the dignity of treating them as adults, while quietly recognising some of their unmet infant needs. These needs might include praise and reassurance, but they are quick to feel patronised by unmerited praise.

In Years 7 and 8 unobtrusive support is often taken up and a bond formed between support staff and the students. However, for some, spending part of the week at an FE college or a youth project can bring the student back to education. The opportunity to do alternative examinations which can be built up from a foundation stage can give these students externally credited evidence of success. The youth service access courses accredited by the City & Guilds of London. Young men and women are often more familiar with this logo on the vans of tradesmen than the logos of the various GCSE awarding bodies!

These students perhaps present the biggest challenge to schools because they are part of a cycle of disaffection. Their parents are more likely to accept the fact that they do not attend school regularly, and some schools are eager to formalise their exclusion in order to lower their truancy figures. In school they know their power to cause disruption; out of school they know that they can disappear from schemes and centres, etc. However, if they slip through the net they might well end up with lifelong social exclusion.

Strategies

There are many forms of emotional and behavioural difficulty that cause acting out behaviour that I have not covered. There are those who act out while going through a traumatic event in their lives; there are those who succumb to peer pressure and those who develop mental illness at puberty. However, the strategies that work for those with ADD often benefit the learning of all pupils.

One of the major strategies involves increasing self-esteem. One way of increasing self-esteem is to have finished pieces of work in the folder. The strategies I usually recommend are these:

- give clear, concise instructions, with as few sub-parts as possible;
- avoid repetitive (boring) tasks;
- tasks should be broken down into small, achievable steps;
- initially tasks should be relatively short;
- academic targets (work completion and understanding) are preferable to behavioural targets;
- focus on desirable behaviour rather than 'don'ts';
- use the 'deadman' test – if a dead person could do it, it isn't behaviour (e.g. I want total silence!);
- give specific and frequent feedback on behaviour;
- small, immediate rewards are more effective than long-term, delayed rewards;
- negative consequences should be clearly focused and highly specific;
- it is better to say, 'now answer question 2' than just 'get on with your work';
- preferred activities, e.g. playing a computer game or shooting baskets, are more effective than sweets or merit cards;
- rewards can be negotiated with the student;
- 'priming' the student; this involves previewing the task with the pupil and speculating what completion will be like;
- interaction with the student should be brief, calm and quiet, and private, with direct eye contact;
- avoid signs of exasperation and 'I have told you "x" times before' – give every reprimand as if it is the first time;
- students with behaviour problems work best in pairs rather than groups;
- when the behaviour is linked with SpLD, dyspraxia, poor attendance, it might be good to offer an alternative to writing as an outcome, e.g. taping a report, a poster or a diagram; otherwise the teaching assistant can work as an amanuensis.

For the sake of the safety of all students and staff in the school it is important that students who cannot control their impulses, and students whose entrenched attitude precludes their following even reasonable rules, are always supported by a second adult in the classroom during Science, Technology and any other lesson where there might be danger. It is important also to be sure that conflicts from outside are not brought into the classroom and students are not subjected to bullying. A teaching assistant circulating in the classroom can be useful in picking up undercurrents of conflict. However, this must be done sensitively and discreetly so that the behaviours are not driven underground, or into remote and secret corners of the school. The patrolling of the school is important for the protection of impulsive students and those vulnerable to bullying.

The link with the home is also important. However, for these students this is sometimes very difficult. A SENCO in a northern secondary school devised the following system when dealing with a boy with AD/HD. She produced three laminated cards, the size of credit cards, in red, orange and green. Each had just one word on it: 'Remember!' The boy was to place it on his desk as soon as he sat down in the classroom. Ostensibly it was to remind him of the behaviours they had discussed. It served a dual purpose of reminding staff that this was a boy who needed support, understanding and gently cueing to keep going with his work. Staff were supplied with slips of paper on which they wrote briefly any problem that he caused during their lesson. These were left in a box for the SENCO and would influence which card he took home that evening. Green meant no further action needed, orange meant that a parent should make an appointment to talk with the SENCO, red meant that his parent should accompany him to school next time he came in. Red was required on two occasions, one of which was when his mother had forgotten to give him his medication. This system could be used with almost any student with a cooperative parent(s).

It is also extremely important to pick up on any interest that the student has and exploit that to the full. It is better to be flexible with the curriculum than to have the student either manipulate his or her exile from the room, or orchestrate a disruptive incident. For most students support is provided to enable them to access the curriculum. The best support for students with acting out EBD is to make sure that the classroom offers something of interest for most of the day.

Conclusion

I feel that students with emotional and behavioural difficulties are the most difficult students to support in mainstream, since they can affect the learning of others. Some students gain a great deal from being taught in small groups, either on or off site. It is important to record incidents of challenging behaviour and examples of cooperative behaviour. It is also important to bear in mind that the most aggressive and difficult students might also be dealing with feelings of deep depression. For those who are constantly being reprimanded at home and at school, and for those who feel rejected at home and at school, self-esteem becomes very low. For those who, because of the culture at home or because of a neurological disability, feel very different from those around them, the school environment can feel very hostile and uncomfortable. If it is decided to transfer them to more suitable provision, this is better done proactively, rather than being left to be a reaction to exclusion from school.

These students often react adversly to the curriculum, the people they are with, and the routine of the school in ways that cannot be ignored. They are the youngsters who are likely to be excluded from school, and, if effective intervention is not available, they and their families are vulnerable to social exclusion.

Further reading

Bennethan, M. and Boxall, M. (2001) *Effective Intervention in Primary Schools: Nurture Groups*, 2nd edn. London: David Fulton Publishers. (This book is about early years but the philosophy is relevant to all those with infant needs of whatever age.)

Carroll, A. and Robertson, M. (2000) *Tourette's Syndrome: a Practical Guide for Teachers, Parents and Carers*. London: David Fulton Publishers.

Cole, J., Visser, J. and Upton G. (1998) *Effective Schooling for Pupils with Emotional and Behavioural Difficulties*. London: David Fulton Publishers.

Cooper, P and O'Regan, F. J. (2001) *Educating Children with AD/HD: A Teacher's Manual*. London: Routledge Falmer.

Garner, P. (1999) *Pupils with Problems*, chaps. 6, 7, 8. Stoke-on-Trent: Trentham Books.

Hook, P. and Vass, A. (2000) *Creative Pastoral Care in Secondary Schools: Effective Inclusion for Difficult Pupils*. London: David Fulton Publishers.

Jordan, R. and Jones, G. (1999) *Meeting the Needs of Children with Autistic Spectrum Disorders: An Introductory Handbook for Practitioners*. London: David Fulton Publishers.

CHAPTER 7

Supporting and Understanding the Invisible or Sad Student in the Classroom

Chapter 6 was about those students who are vulnerable to being excluded from school. This chapter is also about students with emotional and behavioural difficulties, but those who often remain invisible. Towards the end of their school life they may simply remove themselves from school and exclude themselves from a place where they felt themselves to be very minor stakeholders. There are many parallels between chapters 6 and 7 as different students have different methods of dealing with the same problems. The main difference is probably that one group has a high, unmissable profile in the classroom, whereas the profile of the other students is so low that some teachers have referred to them as RHINOS (those really here in name only).

However, those who offer patient, skilled support to these students will often be rewarded with tangible success. Some of these students have always been quiet, unobtrusive members of their classes, but some have become so over the years. For some it might be a very temporary state, following bereavement, family break up, illness or moving from a familiar school to a large unfamiliar one.

Just as in the last chapter I was tempted to use the pronoun 'he', in this chapter it would be easy to use 'she'. However, there are students of each gender within both groups of students with Emotional and Behavioural Difficulties.

Classroom support

Unless these students have a discrete learning, physical or sensory difficulty, it is unlikely they will be allocated support within the classroom. These are sometimes extremely needy students who are 'virtually' excluded, since they engage so little with the cut and thrust of classroom life. Acting out students often have a support teacher 'velcroed' to their side. One head teacher, who asked if she would accept a student who was known to be disruptive, replied: 'I suppose I might have to but I would insist that a "minder" was available all the time.'

This is never likely to be the case with the quiet, withdrawn student. Although some of the quiet students with emotional difficulties rarely hand in a completed piece of work, they remain invisible to all except the most sensitive teachers. It is unlikely that they will solicit the help of a teaching assistant, but might be really pleased if offered help. In the stress of many classrooms individual attention is given as a reaction to an incident or an assertive request, rather than proactively to students who are quietly struggling.

Could it possibly be Attention Deficit Disorder (ADD)?

In the previous chapter I wrote at length about ADD with hyperactivity. One would have to have lived on another planet for the past five years to have missed frequent stories in the media about children with AD/HD. On the other hand teachers on INSET days are often surprised to learn that at least half of children with ADD have it without hyperactivity. The ratio of children with AD/HD is three to four boys to one girl; the ratio of those without hyperactivity is equal numbers of boys and girls.

When a child is diagnosed with AD/HD questions are often asked about siblings. Often a boy's sister is very different; she is described as being quiet, forgetful, always in a daydream, and having problems with doing her work at school. The teacher often ponders about the child who is quiet but often is not doing what the rest of the class is doing. This child rarely finishes the work and yet learns to read and does not seem to lack ability. Because of attentional problems they are often forgetful and arrive without PE gear or their pencil case.

ADD has been defined as:

inability to maintain effort over time in order to meet task demands.
(1996 Report of a Working Party of the British Psychological Society)

This creates enormous problems for the student in the classroom. At a multidisciplinary conference on ADD at Birmingham University in September 1998, young people spoke of the difference a diagnosis had made to their lives. A girl with non-hyperactive ADD spoke of always realising that she was underperforming but not knowing why. She said it was as if there was always a barrier, 'a bit like a net curtain', between her and the completion of a task.

If these students are identified, whether they are medicated or not, they can be supported in the classroom to continue with a task. The strategy of organising pieces of work into small tasks (Chapter 6, page 91) will work well, especially if there is a teaching assistant to cue them from one task to the other. Mark was a boy of average to above average ability but was referred to by classmates as 'the space traveller'. In the United States students with this disorder are often known as 'space cadets!' Often when I looked over his shoulder I saw him doing excellent work, but his intricate diagram of the human heart was being executed in his History book, or he was copying Maths homework into his French book. He needed support in deciding on a way to organise his books so that each subject was distinctive. A short period of support, similar to that given to dyslexic and dyspraxic students (Chapter 5, pages 72–74) can really help students with ADD to gain confidence in organising their work.

These students respond well to medication as it is their inability to concentrate, or focus, which causes them to underachieve. Some teachers have reported dramatic changes in handwriting and presentation of work after a few days on medication. The medication gives them a window of opportunity to gain confidence in their abilities. Unlike the students with AD/HD who are a 'pain in the class' (Cooper 1996) these students are often invisible to the teacher and ignored by their peers. If they do not receive intervention and understanding of their condition they can be prone to depression as they proceed through the school. When the emphasis is on examination success, they are prone to despair as they know that there is something wrong with their ability to learn. It is very important that they be recognised as soon as possible in the secondary school.

Autism and Asperger syndrome

Some students with Asperger syndrome are disruptive because they are frustrated, annoyed and bewildered by much of what is going on around them. However, there are students with autism, especially Asperger syndrome, who stand out for their 'quaintness' rather than their expression of anger. Because they take everything that is said so literally they are often baffled by the behaviour and reactions of others around them. The teacher tells the whole class to 'pull up your socks', most of the girls wear tights, and none of the boys obey, and yet the teacher does not react to having his instruction ignored!

It is very important to put emphasis on what the student is doing right and what has been accomplished. This is where a quiet word from support staff during a lesson can give real encouragement. The student with autism finds it very difficult to cope with a change to routine. Any supply teacher taking the class should have a sheet of printed information and, if possible, the student should be warned that the class will be taken by a supply teacher that day. The problems this can cause will be greatly alleviated if a familiar teaching assistant is in the room.

It is important that the support staff are alert to any bullying that might occur, as well as misunderstandings caused by the autistic young person's tendency to take everything literally. A young girl was beaten up by three others in a cloakroom. They told her that they would get her every day. She was new to the school and thought this must be part of the routine. She presented herself in the same cloakroom every day but her protagonists were not there. Eventually the day came when they were there so she asked them why they had not come on other days. They were totally bewildered to realise that not only had she taken the threat seriously but she had seen the punishment as inevitable. There are now a number of autistic authors who have opened their 'alien' world to us (Williams 1999, O'Neill 1999, Sainsbury 2000 (see Further reading)). They have written books that are easy, compulsive reading and which should be available to any support staff who are supporting students within the autistic spectrum. O'Neill writes as an autistic (*sic*) person, and expresses in this poem some of the feelings of self-containment and acuity of all the senses:

> A child encapsulated
> Her inner world of music,
> sensations luscious honey,
> spicy-rich-warm cinnamon
> a sanctuary of soft movements
> Rocking body
> fingers floating before deep eyes
> feet wandering in soothing circles
> Serene in autistic quiet
> Serene eyes
> Serene hands
> Happy
> Living in her simple coloured box.
> Her blown glass world
> Home
> Self-enclosed dream child
> Toe-steps her own exotic rhythm
> She shields the egg of her universe
> with wide wings.

I interviewed a 12-year-old girl on the day that her parents had been told that she had Asperger syndrome. When I asked her about friends she replied: 'I don't really have any friends. I don't need them. I enjoy being on my own.'

She then spoke to me in detail about how she rushed up to her bedroom when she returned from school. Having collected a snack from the fridge she would sit on her bed and think. She mused about how the thoughts actually came to her head and how one thought led to another. She explained how she thought about thinking. When asked what she most enjoyed at school she replied firmly: 'helping in the office at lunch-time.'

The SENCO had realised how difficult the playground was for this sensitive girl and had arranged for her to spend this time in the school office. Her parents said that she often expressed a desire to attend the same special school as her younger autistic brother, because there were fewer students and 'no one would bump into you.'

A young person with an autistic spectrum disorder can interpret a touch on the shoulder as a push or a blow. Because she was a quiet pensive girl she had not been identified as having special needs in her inner city primary school, although she did not mix with others and was failing to learn. In common with many children on the autistic spectrum she was aloof, keeping others at arm's length and avoiding being close to anyone. She had a normal, lively and charming three-year-old sister, of whom her mother said: 'It is so sad for Georgia. She loves people and wants everyone to love her but the other two don't even seem to notice her. They took no interest when I brought her home from hospital and still only talk to her and join in a game if she makes them.'

Other autistic children are passive, rarely initiating conversations or activities, but joining in when asked. Others can display active but odd behaviour. They often have an overweening enthusiasm for something such as a football team, a transport system or an activity such as fishing. They will talk about this to whoever will listen (initially) and fail to pick up body language that indicates that the other person has had enough. They need support in understanding how others feel, and the importance of two-way communication. Some FE colleges and voluntary organisations have social skills courses where role play and social stories are used to help autistic young people with communication.

Sad children

Some children become sad as the result of unmet emotional needs over a long period, or a trauma involving loss. Exceptional stress can also be responsible. Because young children are so resilient, and even after the death of a loved parent can, between periods of intense grief, run about and laugh with their friends, adults do not always recognise their despair or become aware of a changed pattern of sleep.

Emotional well-being is greatly influenced by the child's early experience. Regrettably there are children whose experience in their early years is worse than anything most adults can imagine. Quiet words from an adult can mean more to these students that they are able to show. Support staff can be effective in making sure that these withdrawn, or unforthcoming youngsters, feel included without jollying them along to take part in any shared activity before they feel ready.

Refugee children

Some of these children arrive in this country with parents or other relatives. However, a large number arrive on their own, sent by parents out of war-torn zones where their lives are in extreme danger. Not only do they arrive in a foreign country completely alone, but they have the added concern about what is happening to their parents and any siblings who might have been left behind. Sometimes it is through art that they can initially express their feelings. There is a case for art therapists to be available in schools where there is a significant intake of refugee children.

Although Britain might have been the destination of choice because of the language, even this will be used differently. We cannot begin to imagine the bewilderment of those who arrive without knowledge of English. These children arrive with minds full of the horrors they have left behind and no adults to help them process the experience until they can be linked with community groups elsewhere in UK. Although a refugee organisation will be involved, support can be sought within the school community where even a teacher, governor or administrator with some knowledge or experience of the mother country can befriend the student. If it is the day of a religious festival in the community from which the student comes, a small card and greeting would make him or her feel included and cared for.

It is vital to make sure that refugee students are not victimised or bullied in the playground, and other unsupervised spaces. Unfortunately, xenophobic feelings whipped up by some sections of the popular media can have an influence on adolescents. Although the need for English as an Additional Language (EAL) does not officially come under Special Educational Needs, in some authorities it is still administered from the same office. Support from the EAL teacher can be useful for the student and staff since the EAL teacher will have experience in this situation.

The refugees who have shown resilience and determination in excelling in their studies within a few years of their arrival are the exception rather than the rule. Many will struggle with a different curriculum, and a very different style of delivery as well as a different language. Again, splitting projects into manageable tasks and cueing each task will prevent the student from becoming overwhelmed. There is usually an enormous will to learn.

Post Traumatic Stress

There are children who are not refugees but who have experienced tragedy or trauma closer to home. Many children in Northern Ireland have spent their whole lives living in a war zone. For those who have suffered bereavement and injury as a result of the troubles, outlook and expectations change. Although this might result in anger that is expressed in the comparative safety of the classroom, teachers report tired and sad children. In areas where people live for periods of time in a state of high alert, children's sleeping patterns can change dramatically, and they are also prone to developing anxiety disorders. This might manifest itself by tearfulness, nail-biting, hair twisting or a 'frozen watchfulness'.

Children who have been in any incident where there has been serious injury or loss of life will also need support. The phenomenon of guilt at having survived when others died has been recognised in young children and adolescents. Students who have suffered these things might benefit from individual counselling or a well-led support group.

In class they might well have difficulty in concentrating and experience some memory loss. If this is recognised, support can be given to help them from task to task, and to jot down anything that needs to be remembered. The healing might take some time but recognition of the problem takes the pressure off the student.

Physical and sexual abuse

For abused children, detachment is often a way to survive: the only way to survive when you are regularly being beaten by a parent whom you love. Being submissive and denying one's own needs can prevent physical abuse but causes psychological harm. The anger that is directed inwards by these children leads them to display anxiety in the safe haven of school, although that can become dangerous if they fear being persuaded into disclosure. This applies also to sexual abuse, especially within or connected closely to the family.

To support these students it is important to make them feel likeable for their own sakes. Make sure any praise given is realistic and related to a specific piece of work or action, otherwise it will seem patronising. Some of us can be impatient for the student to disclose so that the perpetrator can be stopped and punished and so that the student can begin to recover. However, if this has been going on for sometime it is important that the scene is set for possible disclosure so that the student is safe, and has someone available with whom to talk. In a case some years ago, where the student disclosed ongoing abuse by a brother, the authorities were contacted and the mother brought in as a witness. Under this dramatic pressure the student denied having said anything and accused the teacher of 'fancying' her and making all this up. Except for the teacher being asked to help the police with their enquiries nothing else could be done! Many years later, after a major breakdown, a divorce and a period in therapy, the student returned to apologise to the teacher whose help she had been unable to take since it involved betraying her family.

Teachers and support staff are often very aware when a student is suffering abuse, but they need expert support themselves. Now that there is a child protection officer in each school, hopefully the result of any disclosure can be more carefully planned.

Bereavement

Most teachers at some time support a student through the death of a loved grandparent. Unfortunately, students often lose parents and siblings in accidents or because of serious illness. In the case of a long, drawn out terminal illness, the student often needs the most support when it first becomes evident that the outcome could be death. It is important to recognise the student's fears and not give quick reassurances that all will be well. Although this might be the case, this minimises a student's feelings and if they are grounded in fact gives that young person nowhere else to go. Very often, when a parent or sibling finally dies of cancer or another terminal illness, the student has already mourned for the real person and the death of the ill person who has lived a half-life of pain and drugs for weeks or months is initially a relief. It is after the funeral that the mourning for the real person returns but it is important that until then the student is not thought feelingless for showing relief immediately after the bereavement. 'Some children see school as a haven of normality in contrast to the trauma and upset at home' (Mallon 1999).

Grief makes it difficult to concentrate, and for some students this might affect their work for a very long time. If the death has been sudden and unexpected the effect will be more traumatic, and can cause concerns about one's own mortality. Just as in other traumatic situations, children can feel guilty following bereavement. Often the adults around them are too consumed with their own grief to be able to comfort the young people in the family.

It is important for the school to be in touch with the family at such times. The school can also provide support by preparing the other students for the return of the bereaved student. Just as adults often avoid bereaved friends, so do children unless they have positive guidance. It is important that the bereaved student can take their time, but also not be criticised for still telling jokes or laughing at their friends' jokes. They have to feel safe enough for their emotions to be accommodated, since these emotions will be new and unfamiliar. There should be someone available to talk to should the student become overwhelmed in school.

Schoolchildren sometimes, as a class, or a Year, have to be supported through the death of one of their contemporaries. Adolescence is a time of thinking about life, and death, and what happens after death, and they will need to be able to talk about this. In a faith school this might be easier, but in any school it is good to have someone who is trained in bereavement counselling and can give support at this time.

Depression

Depression in children and young people is now recognised. For the student this can be a deep pain and feeling of isolation. It can be caused by a number of factors such as:

- bereavement;
- death of a loved pet;
- moving house to a different area;
- transfer from junior to secondary school;
- fear of failure;
- sudden or chronic bad health (see Chapter 9)
- illness in the family.

Unmet early needs may lead to a predisposition to depression. Children who have been separated from their parent during early years seem to be more prone to depression, as are the children of depressed mothers. It is not known conclusively if this is for genetic or situational reasons.

Adolescents who are depressed may have suicidal thoughts and some do attempt suicide. Also, because adolescence is a period of mood swings, some suicide attempts might be impulsive, and attempts must be taken seriously.

For such adolescents their contact with their peer group is a crucial factor. The adolescent who has a supportive peer group will be helped greatly by them. It is important, however, for the school to make sure that the adolescents who give this support have support themselves and are not consumed by the problems of one of their number who might well need professional help. The adolescent who has no peer network lacks something extremely important.

All students who make suicide attempts, however flawed, should be referred for professional help, preferably help that is designed for that age group.

Parents often do not recognise a child's depression even though sleep and eating habits might have completely changed.

Eating disorders

At any time there will be girls, and possibly boys in a school, with eating disorders. Often it is the teachers who notice the dramatic loss of weight after a holiday, or when teaching a student after not doing so for a year, rather than the parent who sees the student every day. Often students go to a trusted teacher to express their concerns about one of their number who they know is not eating. As a researcher I attended a meeting about a girl who was giving cause for concern because of her truancy, her failure to hand in work and her offhand manner when asked to participate in a lesson. The SENCO commented on how gaunt the girl had become. The PE teacher suddenly recollected two girls telling her that Clare never went into dinner nor brought a packed lunch. The head of year recollected her mother ringing to say that Clare refused her breakfast because she claimed to eat a doughnut at break and a huge lunch with chips. Due to the pressure of work, none of the staff had shared their knowledge with each other. It transpired that Clare's dad had a promoted position the other end of the country and was only returning home at weekends, and her mother was stressed with trying to sell the house and convincing the children that they would make new friends.

Students with eating disorders often truant: the anorexics to avoid eating, and the overweight to avoid PE and teasing by other students. Although in schools we worry about those with anorexia and bulimia more than those who are overweight, all are signs of inner need. Anorexics and bulimics need referring on to specialist agencies before their lives are endangered. However, the staff in a school can support those who are overweight by building their self-esteem. It is important not to join in with the adolescents with thoughtless teasing and name-calling. Trying to enforce a change of diet in school can often drive comfort eating underground and make it worse. First of all the adolescent needs to be accepted on the same terms as other students without the body image getting in the way.

One head teacher did this by making sure that the overweight students were split between just two of the five streams so that none would be alone in the class. There are few students with Prader Willi disorder in mainstream secondary schools, since this is also a learning disorder. However, students with Prader Willi do not have any control over their appetites and will eat any food (or sometimes non-food) that happens to be available. They will sometimes steal it from other students' lunchboxes, not out of dishonesty but from insatiable appetite. They are a very separate case and their treatment will be supervised by specialists in this disorder (see Further reading, Waters 1999).

Children with eating disorders will normally not be children who have needed learning support. Often they are high achievers and will not have given any cause for concern over their social behaviour at school. They need continuous positive feedback and systematic support for what they do at school. Their self-esteem must be boosted and teachers must be vigilant that they are not suffering any teasing or unwanted comments about their body shape. The Food Technology teacher might be helpful in talking them through their anxieties about food in an informed and rational manner.

Shyness

I include shyness in this chapter since for some adolescents it is a cause for concern. However, for others there is a reluctance to draw attention to themselves in school but they are able to socialise at youth clubs and other outside groups. The aspect of shyness often noticed in secondary schools is unforthcomingness. This is different from withdrawal. When asked something or invited to join in the student will normally comply but will not actually put herself (or sometimes himself) forward. Sometimes it is a fear of blushing if asked to do something in front of the class. There are a few people for whom this a real problem, for which medical intervention is available when they are older. Sometimes shyness covers up a fear of failure and the student who has difficulty with work but is too shy to ask can easily be ignored. The shy adolescent sometimes fears criticism and rejection by peers, so keeps a very low profile. As in so many of these 'silent EBDs', it is important to build up confidence and self-esteem. This has to be done quietly, without drawing unwanted attention to the student. If a shy student is dragged into the limelight this can cause great stress.

School phobia

This is a serious EBD which illustrates extreme fear, and is very disruptive for the individual affected, and their family. This student will show signs of extreme anxiety, or even panic, when it is time to go to school, or even when school is discussed. Sometimes these young people complain of illness and undergo medical tests and scans, rather than go to school. Sometimes the young people simply withdraw from school but continue to see their peers. In other cases they withdraw from all peer contact. There is little support the school can give during non-attendance, except to keep in touch. Some feel that to send work home sets a seal of approval on the behaviour but it is far more stressful for the student to return having missed a huge chunk of work. If the problem is with the peers, then having to come into school to fetch and return work might 'keep the door open'.

Strategies

One of the most important ways to support these students is to look out for any sign that others might be bullying them, humiliating them or causing them discomfort in other ways. Sometimes other staff, in trying to jolly them along might be inadvertently adding to their feeling of fear and isolation. Otherwise it is important to:

- find time to talk to the pupil in a relaxed manner;
- use quiet, realistic praise and encouragement;
- make sure the student is not humiliated in a group situation;
- find out interests and strengths and plan for success in the curriculum;
- pair with another student for some work;
- peer tutoring (the tutor gains in self-esteem and both gain from companionship);
- consider the playground environment; if necessary provide unobtrusive adult support;

- when asking questions around the class allow nervous children to 'pass and nominate' (they nominate someone who they think can answer the question but who has not answered for the last 'n' turns; nominating can make them popular with others and shows whether they are aware of the rest of the class);
- find jobs they can do for adults or younger children within the building during some lunch-times, e.g. Sophie helped in the school office.

Conclusion

Some of these problems are transitory and are related to a specific event or situation, such as moving to secondary school. Some students who were considered a bit immature at primary school, but were, on the whole happy and accepted, find transition to a large secondary school very difficult. This is alleviated in some schools by having just the Sixth Form (Years 12 and 13) and the incoming students (Years 7, 8 or 9) in for the first day.

In one school sixth formers are trained to be 'buddies' to individual incoming students who have been identified in their feeder schools as being vulnerable. These students might have learning or behavioural needs, or they might have suffered bereavement, or have a stressful home situation.

In another school there is an ABC (All Busy Club) run by two teaching assistants three lunch-times a week for any Year 7 boys who do not want to be in the playground. They can do their homework, play board games or engage in other projects together. Vulnerable students from other age groups are invited to come in to help.

Roots of prosocial, considerate behaviour lie in early family experiences. However, as children grow up peer relationships become more important. Even the most isolated and withdrawn student may well wish to be part of a group and develop defensive behaviour rather than admit this. These are often the last students to be chosen for teams and it is better to look as if one does not care than to accept rejection.

Teachers and support staff working with invisible and sad students are often walking on eggshells since adolescents with such great personal sensitivity can often show resentment of the most well-meaning approaches. Some adolescents are so damaged by their life histories that professional help may be needed.

Further reading

Alsop, P. and McCaffrey, T. (eds) (1993) *How to Cope with Childhood Stress: A Practical Guide for Teachers.* Harlow: Longman.

Chazan, M. *et al.* (1998) *Helping Socially Withdrawn Adolescents.* London: Cassell.

Kinchin, D. and Brown, E. (2001) *Supporting Children with Post Traumatic Stress Disorder.* London: David Fulton Publishers.

Mallon, B. (1998) *Helping Children to Manage Loss.* London: Jessica Kingsley Publishers.

O'Neill, J. (1999) *Through the Eyes of Aliens: A Book about Autistic People.* London: Jessica Kingsley Publishers.

Powell, S. (ed.) (2000) *Helping Children with Autism to Learn.* London: David Fulton Publishers.

Sainsbury, C. (2000) *Martian in the Playground.* Bristol: Lucky Duck Publishing.

Smith, H. (1995) *Unhappy Children: Reasons and Remedies.* London: Free Association Books.

Smith, S. C. (1995) *The Forgotten Mourners: Guidelines for Working with Bereaved Children*, 2nd edn. London: Jessica Kingsley Publishers.

Waters, J. (1999) *Prader-Willi Syndrome: A Practical Guide.* London: David Fulton Publishers.

Williams, D. (1999) *Like Colour Blind.* London: Jessica Kingsley Publishers.

CHAPTER 8

Supporting Students with Sensory and Physical Difficulties in Mainstream Classrooms

Sensory impairment

Students with sensory impairment are more likely to be supported by a specialist in the classroom than other students so far described. Although an increasing number of these students are now coping very successfully in mainstream classrooms, there is still room for debate in individual cases as to whether it is the best place for all students with these difficulties. Unless the disability is the result of an accident or illness during childhood, these students will have received special provision throughout their childhood.

There are a number of students with these difficulties who will also have the learning and behavioural difficulties described in earlier chapters. The behavioural difficulties might well be because of their physical or sensory difficulties. In my research I visited the family whose daughter had been born at 29 weeks, weighing less than a kilogram. She had extremely bad sight and had little movement in the right side of her body. She was in mainstream school with little support and had a totally 'can do' attitude to life, only agreeing to use a wheelchair for short periods after leg surgery. She was in the second of four streams at her comprehensive school and had a number of close friends. She was doing particularly well in modern foreign languages. She was driving her teachers and her family mad with her constant desire to be reassured.

The importance of liaison with specialist advisers and consultants

Most of the children will have had their visual and their hearing problems diagnosed during their early years and their progress will have been monitored by the qualified teachers of the deaf and the visually impaired.

These same people might well have taught them when they were younger, or have done much to support their education in their primary school. Qualified teachers in these special needs and therapists will also have made sure that any aids which they need are available and are kept in good order. The support, expertise, experience and energy of these experts is of paramount importance when a hearing or visually impaired student is integrated into any school. In primary school liaison is easier to achieve as most children are taught by just one teacher. In secondary school it is more difficult as any child might be taught by ten or more teachers on a regular basis. The SENCO will be the one to meet the specialist and then liase with the staff.

It is important that the subject teachers know that expert help is available. The Science or Modern Language teachers might find it helpful to be able to consult them about problems specific to their subject or their teaching environment. If the peripatetic teacher cannot fully solve the problems, they may be able to contact other colleagues who have had long experience in specialist schools.

When students with visual difficulties move into secondary school it is important that a specialist is aware of the environment and can discuss any changes or pitfalls before the student transfers from primary school. During my first research a retired headmaster of a school for the visually impaired supported students during their first weeks in secondary school. Now all except two students with VI are in one secondary school. A full-time teacher of the visually impaired is based there and goes from there to advise the other two schools. They also share facilities such as the Braille machine and large print set texts. By the time the student begins at secondary school the specialist will be well known in the staff room.

There are some situations which are only learnt with experience. The school that accommodates most of the students with VI laid bright white lines throughout all the corridors, just as they have in schools for VI. There are far fewer students in these schools and floor strips that had lasted a year in these schools lasted less than six weeks in an environment where over a 1,000 students changed lessons five times a day. The rubberised 'paint' used to put lines on roads might be more appropriate! Handrails had also been provided but often the handrail gave way to a group of students standing against it while waiting to enter a class.

It is vital that secondary school teachers and support staff have the opportunity to attend relevant INSET. It is important for teachers to be familiar with the aids students use and to be aware of classroom practices that might put some students at a disadvantage. For example, do all teachers realise that if they stand with their backs to a window, a child who relies on lip-reading will have greater difficulty seeing their mouth, and they will disappear altogether for the child who is visually impaired. These INSETs are also an opportunity for teachers to meet the specialists so that they know who to approach for advice later.

The role of support staff

Where the student has normal learning ability, but needs help with aids, a specially trained non-teaching assistant, such as an NNEB (recognised by the Nursery Nurses Enrolment Board) provides very appropriate support. In some cases the support from primary school moves up into secondary school with the student. In one school the supporter of a boy with spina bifida also took on the support of a boy wheelchair-bound with 'brittle bones'. She accompanies both boys to lessons as they have been placed in the same teaching group. There is no need for her to stay and she will only return at the teacher's request. However, in practical lessons she is essential for holding apparatus and reaching items from shelves, etc. She has to be careful only to act on instructions from the boys and leave the decision-making to them. One of the main skills she needs is to be able to do nothing until asked so that she does not make either boy more dependent on her than he need be. The boy who requires intimate physical help is beginning to be eager to manage more of this for himself. Breaktimes are short and it would be quicker for the assistant to do everything for him. However, part of her support function must be to support his growing independence, even though she knows the early results might not always be perfect.

Supporting students with physical impairment in secondary schools is an extremely sensitive task. In one school there are two girls, in different years, with cerebral palsy which hampers their hand movements. Both expressed resentment that the teaching assistant who was there for them in Textiles and Food Technology lessons was often too busy helping others with spellings, etc., to be available when they needed needles threading or onions chopping (see Chapter 2). This meant they fell behind the rest of the class with their preparation, which was only solved by the TA completing the task, the bit they could have done, given time, at the end of the lesson. It is very difficult for a TA to remain available when there are insistent requests for help elsewhere but this is the intention of the statement provision.

Sally, a visually impaired girl, refused to accept help from support in the classroom, so a member of the office staff accepted extra hours to anticipate her needs. She magnified copies of work sheets, obtained large print books and tapes from the library and was in the vicinity when Sally emerged from lessons. She satisfied the safety requirements of the school without interfering with Sally's desire to do things herself. Sally made sure she always had a friend with whom she could link arms, a valuable strategy which would serve her well in the outside world.

Students with hearing difficulties

The support of a student in a school where there is a hearing impaired unit is totally different from that in a school where a single child is being supported. This book does not intend to cover the expert support which is given by those who specialise in the education of HI students.

Support staff might be asked to work with a student whose intermittent hearing loss was just one item on the list of difficulties on the statement. One girl with intermediate hearing loss had the monotone indistinct speech often connected with much more severe hearing loss. She had permanent grommets in both ears, but denied that there was any problem with her hearing and stubbornly refused to sit near the front of the class. She was 14 and had fought back against years of mockery by her peers and, presumably, the frustration of not always knowing what was going on. She always aligned herself with the high achievers in her class and copied their work. She produced beautiful, neat work, but had hardly any understanding of it, and consequently always did badly in examinations. She was extremely depressed and had become very spiteful towards nearly everyone in her class. Some of the girls had been patient with her dependency on them for a number of years, but now she did everything she could to annoy them. Staff were worried about her increasing alienation and her unrealistic ambition to go to university, 'so she could learn to be a clever person'.

Initially she refused my support, always directing me to someone she felt needed my services. The girls who had always helped her were eager for her to accept support as she was hindering them. Eventually she would make use of support that looked as if it was being given to someone else nearby. She would not admit to a hearing difficulty and relied heavily on lip-reading.

She was allocated 45 minutes a week, 1:1 with me, but she tried to avoid this by always coming with a friend whom she said needed help. Eventually I managed to engage her (alone) in a programme of instrumental enrichment (Feuerstein 1978) see pages 55–57. This was unrelated to anything she had done before and therefore there was no risk of her displaying ignorance. It was also necessary to hold a dialogue so there was an opportunity to assess her hearing loss. In eight weeks two instruments were studied: one comprising joining dots to form repeated shapes that were presented at a number of different angles, the other was concerned with orientation within a space. An important element of this programme is linking what is explored in the instruments with the familiar curriculum. It is important for the student to think about the way he or she thinks and how conclusions are reached, to realise when that process is taking place and to acknowledge it with the words 'Just a minute, let me think!'. Staff who taught her reported that she often said to them, 'Ang on, I got to fink abaht it', when she was asked a question or the time came to do written work in class. She became much less impulsive, angry and frustrated, and instead of tearing up work when it did not reach her high expectations, completed the part of the work she was able to do well.

This girl had a behavioural difficulty that was certainly linked with frustration caused by her hearing impairment. She was totally dependent on lip-reading and may well also have had a learning difficulty. She had been a very premature baby whose developmental delay had resulted in her receiving her infant education in a special unit. It was here that her hearing loss had been identified.

In a primary school with a special hearing impaired unit all the children learn British Sign Language from an early age. This leads to good integration in school and in the community. However, one has to be alert to the frustration experienced by hearing impaired and deaf children. Often this is because of the quality of their speech, and because of the indistinct sound they hear through their aids. They are also vulnerable to bullying by other children. This bullying can be subtle and hardly detectable by adults, who might think the bully is a friend or companion. Support staff at schools can be alert to this situation.

The best support the student can receive in school is that teachers make sure their mouths are always clearly visible to the HI student during the lesson, and that background noise is kept to a minimum since the aid magnifies certain tones. There should be liaison before the lesson between the teacher and the support since it will be important that the student receives precise instructions and knows exactly what to do. Often the student will wait until others are halfway through the task before starting. This is not in order to copy but because then they know what is required.

If there is a radio aid to be worn by the teacher it is vital that this is switched on from the beginning of the lesson, and that he or she checks that the student is receiving the sound as well as he or she can. Support staff can gently remind the busy teacher who has forgotten as otherwise the student will miss the vital beginning of the lesson.

Children with visual difficulties

Again, liaison between the specialist teacher and the SENCO will be important so that both the subject teachers and the support staff are fully informed of the nature of the student's difficulty. In some cases of visual difficulty the student has been taught Braille. In other cases there might be an appreciable amount of vision which can be maximised by using close circuit TV. Photocopying and enlarging reading matter will help. It is also well worth experimenting with positions and angles from which to work. The lighting and set out of each classroom will be different so this will have to be assessed in each environment. A student with a reduced field of vision ('tunnel vision') might, in fact benefit from having the print size reduced so that more may be taken in. Others will benefit from having the print enlarged and will best read the chalk board from a closed circuit TV monitor on the desk. One young man at a local grammar school finds the CCTV of great value in following the experiments as well as the board work in Science lessons.

There are some visual defects which are concerned with focusing that permit students to work with the minimum of adaptation and enlargement of materials but entail such increased effort from them that, without frequent breaks, they become very fatigued. A young lady with nystagmus was said by some staff to do good work 'when she wanted to', although she was failing badly in some subjects. These were mainly subjects that were timetabled later in the day when she was suffering from intense tiredness. She was often absent from school with headaches. However, when she was allowed to rest during the day if she felt too tired to continue, and the demands for her to produce exactly the same amount of work as her peers were waived, her attendance improved and she lost some of the impatience which was making her unpopular with staff and pupils. It was agreed only to enter her for GCSE examinations where she could be expected to achieve a C grade or above. Arrangements were made for her to sit in a separate room during the examinations and have half-hour breaks, so she could sit back in an easy chair and rest her eyes. Staff had problems in 1993 with accepting this as full integration; by 2000 they had realised that equal access to the curriculum is the key, and this was being achieved. It is not synonymous with equal input or equal output.

Most of the visually impaired students went to one school that was well resourced for them. However, when I asked the head of one school if he had ever had to accept a statemented student against his will, he quoted the case of an incoming student with little sight. His parents had insisted on him attending the same school as his brothers, which was also the school attended by his father and uncles years before. The head, the SENCO and support staff had misgivings about this student, even though the specialist teacher in the other school had offered support and an arrangement had been made to share Braille and photocopying facilities.

Six weeks later, after the boy had attended for an induction visit, prior to his entry the next term, there was much optimism. The boy had circulated well during the day. He was a robust character who had an easy relationship with the boys with whom he had grown up. He had chosen the school and the school was now happy about supporting him.

Students with mild cerebral palsy or ataxia

During the original research the students with cerebral palsy were coping in old schools with difficult staircases. Since then a new school has been built and opened in 1998. This school has ramps and a lift, and the input from a girl who was among the first intake, and another who followed the year later, is given later in the chapter on page 119.

Physically disabled students often need little support in the classroom unless there are other learning and behavioural difficulties. They do however become very tired because of the extra effort expended just walking from lesson to lesson around a large secondary school, carrying a heavy load of books with them. The provision of support has to be done with great sensitivity. They certainly do not want an assistant permanently at hand but in practical lessons help is often needed because of poor motor control and coordination.

I supported Derek during his transfer from primary to secondary school and up to Year 11, and I have been happy to be a listening ear during his first year at university. He suffered oxygen deprivation shortly after birth, resulting in an uncontrollable tremor in his hands, an awkward gait and difficulty in modulating his voice and in articulating some words. At primary school, because he was unable to write legibly and articulate clearly, his level of ability was not recognised until he won a regional chess competition. His high ability was revealed when he was allocated a laptop computer and small printer and immediately produced excellent work. At 11 he was one of the first students to be allocated a laptop in this borough. Fortunately, now- adays students with his difficulty would have a computer at a much earlier age. My main role in supporting Derek was to liaise with his teachers, and between home and school. It was sometimes difficult to keep his parents' expectations at a realistic level and to help them cope with their son's adolescent anger at his difficulties.

In his first year Derek had suffered from a very subtle, quite sophisticated, form of bullying. Somehow the class had decided that they would elect him form captain for the second half of the second term. He was amazed and extremely flattered to be proposed and said repeatedly, 'I never knew I was so popular'. He felt that even though he did not expect to be elected he would always be pleased to have been nominated. His mother and I were surprised, and not a little anxious to hear that he had been unanimously elected to assume this responsibility, as the form captain read the notices every morning and was responsible for making sure the other boys waited in an orderly fashion outside classrooms. Derek's elation was short-lived, however, as he had to repeat notices over and over again. An ostensibly helpful classmate then suggested he should write them on the board – an impossibility for a boy who did every bit of work on a computer. When the class misbehaved outside classrooms, students said it was because they did not understand what Derek wanted them to do. In this way he was forced to face all his physical weaknesses and became acutely depressed. He immediately began to worry that he would never be able to do any job. Although staff soon realised what had happened and the boys were reprimanded, Derek received support during his remaining time in office but the damage was done. For a while he not only felt he was hopeless but that he had no friends. This was the school's first experience of a physically disabled student and they learnt much from this painful experience.

His physical difficulties became worse with his pubertal growth spurt. He also had a stroke, which caused complete loss of speech and mobility during Year 10. Once he was discharged from hospital he was determined to go back to school. The boys, who had tormented him three years earlier, and teachers made huge, and maybe sometimes unwise, efforts to help him to move between the two floors until the timetable could be adapted. They had visited him in hospital and now made sure that he was included in trips to the town on Saturdays even though it meant taking him in a wheelchair for several months. He has recently accepted the fact that physically he will 'never be more than 70 per cent', and has thrown himself wholeheartedly into studying for a degree in criminal law. Despite his fears as an adolescent, he has a steady girlfriend. He has also trained as a learning mentor to students in a local secondary school.

Support in the classroom

Support for physically disabled students in the classroom will usually entail acting as a pair of hands. It is important to write only what the student would write and to work purely as an amanuensis. In some schools lab technicians and technology technicians can be given extra hours to support the student since they are familiar with the routine of the lab and do not need to sit through the lesson. They can merely be there to hold apparatus. In 1993 this had the added advantage that the other students were used to seeing lab staff around and it did not draw attention to the need for support. Times have changed and students are now totally used to another person in the classroom who is to available to give help when and where needed. Hence Zoe's problem of having to wait for help that had been provided for her, while the teaching assistant responded to the demands of more vociferous students. Another girl with cerebral palsy also complained that she often had to wait so long for help in Food Technology that her food was not cooked by the end of the lesson, while the support staff sorted out other students' problems. One reason for this seemed to be that both girls had soft, fairly indistinct speech and were fairly withdrawn.

In the early days of support I supported a very competent young lady in Chemistry lessons. I was so bad at Chemistry that I often could not understand what Sue wanted me to do. She became frustrated as she thought it was because of her poor articulation rather than my stupidity. Out of guilt for failing her in her hour of need I adopted the role of 'faithful servant' in other things, until one day she barked at me, 'I can do it myself. Go and help someone who can't.' Her parents had insisted on her having the support of a qualified teacher, but she would have received much more appropriate support from the lab technician or TA.

The support Sue needed was purely technical, unlike Ella, another girl with cerebral palsy, who also had learning difficulties. Ella had several long absences from school for major operations on her legs. Because she was used to adult attention in hospital she was enthusiastic in her welcome of classroom support. She needed support in understanding processes in Science, in writing her notes and in actually reading her textbook. Even without CP she would probably need learning support in the classroom. She enjoyed using her laptop and the resultant folder of neat work. She was regarded by everyone in the school as a very special person, cheerfully accepting praise for the effort she puts into her work. By the time of my second visit she had achieved her ambition to work in the school kitchen.

Students in wheelchairs

It is important for students in wheelchairs to be able to move around the school as freely as possible. This might mean teachers making sure that the layout of their rooms allows these students to be as independent as possible in fetching equipment for themselves. The support staff are in an ideal situation to give some thought to this. They can encourage these students to use their elbow sticks if they have them as it is important for them to exercise their limbs. Indeed, students with wheelchairs sometimes push them from lesson to lesson so that it can be used to accommodate their bags. This provides similar exercise and means they can be independent of an assistant to carry the bag.

One young man, Tim, is a pupil in a large mainstream comprehensive school. He has a number of congenital physical problems and on good days can walk from lesson to lesson, but on his worst days cannot even propel his wheelchair. There is a non-teaching assistant available at all times to assist him from lesson to lesson even if it only means carrying his 'booster' cushion. There is no need for the assistant to stay in the lesson but she can detect when he is too weary to continue on the timetable and can retire with him to a quiet room where he can have a rest or do some of the work at his own pace. Since Tim is very small it would be easy for him to be knocked over in the crush when 2,000 students change lessons. However, students know that when they see Mrs Brown, Tim must be there, and they take more care.

Integration does not mean that disabled students have to have precisely the same demands placed upon them as the able-bodied. In a class students' hands are raised to communicate with the teacher or answer questions. Disabled students might not be able to lift their hands, or hold them up for any time. It is important that when the time comes for student participation, the disabled child does not become 'invisible'. Sometimes for full participation in the lesson a sign to be used in these situations has to be agreed between the teacher and the student.

In the playground the support of all the staff in the school will be important to make sure that the student in the wheelchair is not subject to bullying, subtle or otherwise. In this context, well-meaning but patronising help may have to be gently curbed and the instigator given some explanation about why this is hurtful. It is important that other students are not allowed to make wheeling the child into a game unless it is on the specific terms of the child in the chair. It is also important for students to be able to assert themselves and be supported if they say 'No' to something which they have perhaps gone along with previously. Although some disabled students might enjoy being included in the rough and tumble of the playground, it is important for them to have the option of retiring to somewhere quieter. Ideally there should be more than one physically disabled student integrated in any school and a quiet room should be available for them to be together when they are tired, anxious or just feel in need of mutual support.

There is no doubt that many students with physical and sensory disabilities often suffer from tiredness and depression which is the result of their disability, and their greater understanding of its implications as they experience the changes of adolescence. It is vital that they are aware of specialist organisations that provide support and sometimes one-to-one counselling during difficult times. It is important for teachers and support staff to understand when they are sometimes rude and dismissive. Every disabled student I have encountered has expressed fears about future employment and some have confessed to having ambitions they know cannot be realised. Derek went through a stage of wanting to be a stand-up comic or a chef. When Sue was told how easily she would find a post using computers she retorted, 'But I would rather be an air hostess'.

In my recent research I interviewed a boy who had been born with a missing forearm. His teachers and parents stressed that he really had no difficulties and his parents doubted that he would agree to talk to me. When I rang to ask the boy for an appointment he was very eager to talk. He had so many fears about whether he would be able to find employment and whether any girl would want to go out with a boy with one arm. Research ethics meant I could not divulge his fears. However, I spent some time rehearsing with him questions he could ask, and discussing where he could find a listening ear. It is to be hoped that the organisation 'Connexions', which will provide combined services for 13- to 19-year-olds, will be able to provide this kind of help to individuals.

Disabled students and bullying

One of the most difficult problems of integrating these students into mainstream has been that of bullying. Whatever projects or programmes are organised to counteract bullying, there is always a risk that it will happen. The students are often those who have themselves been the victims of bullies, either at school, in their neighbourhoods, or in their families. It is difficult to design a programme to deter a bully who has been bullied by his or her parents for as long as he or she can remember. In a case where a disabled student is being bullied by a student who has been a victim at another time, the problem will not be solved unless the bully also receives some kind of support in gaining insight into his or her behaviour. As illustrated by Derek's story earlier in this chapter, there is also the contagious kind of bullying where one or two of the class begin some unpleasantness and before those in authority are aware of what is happening others are sucked into victimising, isolating and ridiculing a student. This can involve students who would not otherwise have taken part in bullying and are often full of genuine remorse when they realise how they have been influenced to behave.

It is important that the disabled student has someone in whom to confide if bullying occurs. On rare occasions the bully has been an overenthusiastic teacher who feels the student is taking advantage of their special status within the school. Successful support will involve sorting out the problem without alienating the student from his peers or his teachers.

New school, new opportunities, new problems

The new school that has been built with total disabled access is the first choice for almost all parents with physically disabled offspring. Anna, who was in the first intake, and her parents, were consulted over the initial provision. However, they were surprised when the lift was designed to accommodate Anna, her walking frame or wheelchair, and a teaching assistant. This was ideal for the first year but Anna, in common with all adolescents, grew! In the three years that have passed she has moved up three sizes of frame and wheelchair. The lift now accommodates just Anna and her frame, or whichever other disabled student is using it, unless they are still as small as Anna was at eleven. This means that Anna rides up alone. With her frame she has to back out as there is no room to turn. She also states that it is difficult to avoid grazing her knuckles in the manoeuvre. Fortunately she only needed the wheelchair when she was having operations on her legs in earlier years. However, there are heavy fire-doors along the corridor and Anna now realises she relied on the teaching assistant to open these. Now she waits, trapped behind a door until she is missed from her class and someone comes to retrieve her, or someone happens to pass by.

Zoe likes to climb the stairs with her friends but by lunch-time, and sometimes before, she is too tired to do this. Some staff ask her why she uses the lift when she can use the stairs and regard her as taking advantage. The physiotherapist is keen for her to increase her use of her right hand and so has suggested she walks the side of the stairs where she has to use this hand on the banister. This means on certain staircases she is going against the rest of the crowd and very vulnerable to being toppled over.

In the Science labs there are some chairs with backs and others without backs. Anna and Zoe both take longer going from class to class so rarely obtain a chair with a back. Both individually told me how much easier this would make their lives, especially when they had Science in the afternoon.

A well meaning PE teacher is determined that all students should be included but, according to Zoe, 'while the others are going over normal hurdles I am on my own going over ones about six inches from the ground. What is the point?'

Both are fully aware of the feats achieved by athletes in the para Olympics but as Anna says, 'if I am last in every race here, even with a frame, I am hardly going to be an athlete.'

Zoe feels frustrated that she has to have physiotherapy twice a week after school although the physiotherapist is prepared to do it during PE lessons in school. Anna is preparing for GCSEs and feels too tired to complete her homework when she has a physio session after school. However, both girls love the way that the PE teacher has found a way to include them in dance and apparatus work.

I was in the privileged position of being able to listen to the two girls for an hour each, separately. It was interesting that they made the same comments although they were not friends. Both had a wide circle of friends among their peers. Both had been integrated since reception class. Zoe's parents had fought a high profile case, to have her admitted to a mainstream day nursery at the age of three. However, the parents admitted that it had been a constant fight to keep the friendships going since they always had to be transported. Their mothers either went on school trips or nominated a friend or relative to go in their stead.

The head spoke of a physically disabled boy who was unable to mix with others. He made himself unpopular with staff by seeking them out and buttonholing them for conversation, while ignoring and rebuffing any overtures made by his peers. At the sight of a visitor he had wheeled himself out into the middle of the concourse. Unfortunately his parents had not returned a consent form permitting me to interview him. The consensus of staff opinion was that he would be happier in the smaller environment of a special school.

The SENCO had faced a very steep learning curve when first coming to the school but was tackling the job with enthusiasm. Both girls agreed that they enjoyed school and, despite their criticisms, they felt everyone was supporting them as much as possible. Anna had already given her input to planning facilities for the new Sixth Form block.

Conclusion

In writing about the support of special needs it is important to acknowledge that these needs are so diverse that even those who have worked for many years in this field will not have come across every need. Most students have a combination of needs; the disability might cause them some problems of which even those who live close to them are unaware. Students with sensory or physical disability who are in the final year of statutory education are bound to have worries about their future. They might also have worries about their sexual development and whether their needs in this area will be fulfilled. It is important that they have access to people with whom they can discuss this. However well integrated, they will need to be aware of contacts they can make with people with similar difficulties.

There are some useful addresses in the Appendix for those teaching the hearing and visually impaired.

Further reading

Arter C. *et al.* (1999) *Children with Visual Impairment in Mainstream Settings.* London: David Fulton Publishers.

Cornwall, J. (1995) *Choice, Opportunity and Learning: Educating Children and Young People who are Physiacally Disabled.* London: David Fulton Publishers.

Slade, M. (1990) *One Step at a Time.* Wrexham: Maysdale Books.

Varma, V. (ed.) (1996) *The Inner Life of Children with Special Educational Needs.* London: Whurr. Chapter 1 (Corley, G. and Pring, L.) 'The inner life of visually impaired children'. Chapter 2 (Kiff, P. and Bond, D.) 'The inner life of deaf children.' Chapter 3 (Smith, M.) 'The secret life of the physically Disabled Child'.

Watson, L., Gregory, S. and Powers, S. (1999) *Deaf and Hearing Impaired Children in Mainstream Schools.* London: David Fulton Publishers.

CHAPTER 9

Supporting Sick Children in the Classroom

Most teachers during the course of their careers will at some time be aware of a child in the classroom who has medical problems. These might be of a chronic nature such as asthma, diabetes, epilepsy, cystic fibrosis or ME, or a serious illness such as cancer or muscular dystrophy where there is a possibility of the student dying before finishing his or her education.

Despite, or perhaps because of, the complexity of this subject, this will be a short chapter. My main purpose is merely to raise awareness of the feelings of these students, their parents, their siblings and, last but not least their friends. There will be a very full list of Further reading. I shall also refer throughout to *The Education of Children with Medical Conditions* (Closs 2000).

I do not claim to mention every condition which will be encountered in the classroom, however I shall include a few case studies from both research projects. The one condition that every teacher will be aware of is asthma. Roughly one in ten British schoolchildren are diagnosed with this condition in varying degrees of severity. A number of students miss days from school, or come to school tired after a disturbed night.

Home and hospital tuition

In this area of special needs, teachers who have experience of teaching individuals in hospital, and at home will have invaluable expertise and can support teachers in the classroom. Often in the case of a student who has been critically ill, it will be the home tutor who will liaise with the school about the re-entry of the student. In some cases the student will have periods in mainstream interspersed with periods with a home tutor when his or her condition becomes worse, or they have to have surgery.

The home tutor will also know the parents or carers of the student and can share useful knowledge with the class teacher. It is easier to be patient with what seem to be overprotective parents, when one knows what they have been through in another stage of their child's illness. If the student is in and out of school it will be important that the home tutor is given suitable work and resources to maximise the short time he or she will have to educate the student. The home tutor and the form teacher might together discuss how many GCSEs it is realistic to aim for, and what examination privileges should be applied for. Some sick children wish to do their examinations even though they have a life-threatening illness. It might help them to be in a separate room where they can rest for regular periods, or to have special seating arrangements to lessen any physical discomfort they might have.

Case studies

Neil, aged 13, had a severe type of epilepsy which meant that he had up to 20 fits a day. He was in a mainstream classroom. His fits were preceded by a sudden roar, followed by involuntary hand and arm movements for seconds before he regained consciousness. He was in a class of students some of whom he had been with since the age of 5 and his classmates rarely looked up from their work when they heard Neil's roar. The teacher of the class would merely move to him and hold him around the shoulders until the spasm was over. This has happened up to five times in one Maths lesson without the teacher losing her train of thought, and with the students working normally. Nevertheless, it is noticeable that Neil is having more frequent and longer fits as he grows up. This is making him more tired and sometimes, at the end of the lesson a teacher will suggest that Neil needs to go and rest.

Derek's story is in another chapter (Chapter 8). However I mention Derek here because as a result of being in hospital in another authority there was no liaison between his teachers and the hospital tutors. Because he had no speech, the tutor could only converse with Derek by speaking to him and then reading his reply from his laptop screen. Those who knew Derek well found this no barrier to understanding but it was obviously not the ideal way to start a student–tutor relationship. Probably Derek's anxiety about the work he was missing at school made his illness worse. When he returned to school he was determined to do everything but burnt himself out early in the week and was too tired for school on Thursday and Friday. It was then decided that Derek should have an area set aside for a lie down immediately after lunch until start of afternoon school. This worked well.

I spoke to the head of the school before **Claire** was due to start there the following September. She expressed her anxiety about the prospect of having a student who at 11 had a degenerative illness and probably a very shortened lifespan. The main problem was that Claire had in the last six months at primary school lost her sight. Although it was felt she would have been better catered for at the school with a VI specialist, the family had a long tradition of being educated at this school. When I spoke to the SENCO six months after Claire had started school Claire was in hospital. Her condition had suddenly become much worse, involving paralysis first of her limbs, and then of her respiratory tract. She was now critically ill in hospital and not expected to live much longer. However her schoolfriends were regularly being taken 16 miles by their parents to visit her in hospital. She had been much liked and much admired during the four and a half months she had been in the school. There was no suggestion that she should not have come and both the SENCO and the head felt that her presence had added something special to the school. Although the outcome was going to be very sad the staff thought that the girls would cope well as they were doing all they could while she was still able to 'see' them. Burnett (2000), in Closs, writes of home tutoring a girl with a similar condition who died very suddenly. Before she died she said to her tutor: 'I am very afraid I may die but what upsets me most is that no one from my school has written or been to visit me. I feel I don't matter.' Certainly this was not Claire's experience in spite of being in a new school.

Nigel was a very popular boy of 15 who was diagnosed with Hodgkins disease during the long summer holiday prior to going into Year 11. His chemotherapy was started immediately and it was assumed that he would return to school. Although he had always been a very popular character in school he found it very hard to attend once he lost all his hair. One supply teacher told him to remove his baseball cap, and remarked that he should not have had his head shaved if he did not like it. Nigel did not return to school until his hair grew back some three months later. If only the supply teacher had been briefed!

Later he had steroidal treatment that left him bloated and the combination of hating his own body and being called fatty by boys he had always seen as his mates was too much. Although he still went to school he withdrew into himself and pushed away some of the boys who were genuinely wanting to help. He had just one friend, a fairly quiet boy, who stuck with him throughout. The teachers at the school found it difficult to speak about Nigel without becoming tearful because he had gone from being a larger than life, clever boy who could drive them mad as a class clown, to a withdrawn sick child who lost all interest in his friends.

He died the day before he would have gone into the Sixth Form. His constant friend was with him. They had together planned his funeral and disposal of goods. Allan went into school the next day and sat with the priest and head teacher to organise the service. Nigel had chosen boys for the readings and bidding prayers and hymns for the choir. Students who had felt guilty and rejected by their mate were helped by knowing that it meant a great deal to have them take part in his funeral. There is just one boy who ten years later has been unable to move on and still often sits near Nigel's grave, leaving a coke can as a memorial. This illustrates the importance of identifying students who, for a number of reasons, might need support after the death of a peer. Ben had called at the house during the holidays to see Nigel, not realising that he was dying, and had been told he was too tired. Although this was true, Ben had not realised how seriously ill his friend was and felt excluded.

Alice is a 14-year-old girl with cystic fibrosis. Because the school has three students (two siblings) with this condition there is a physiotherapy room where they can have their programme daily. It is the largest school in the borough and has a number of students with medical difficulties. One of the support staff is a qualified nurse who keeps an eye on all students with medical conditions. If she feels Alice is struggling she will obtain work from the teacher and let Alice (or any other similar child) do it in the sick room. Alice is awaiting a lung transplant and is very poorly but her parents can confidently send her to school, knowing that her medical needs are being met.

Diwan aged 16 has had ME (myalgic encephalomyelitis) since he was in Year 8 of his grammar school. The school had experience of a previous student with ME who rarely attended the school and received most of his education from a home tutor. Neither Diwan nor his parents wanted this to happen so from the start of the problems the head teacher obtained funding for a taxi to bring Diwan to school and take him home. It was important that the taxi was not rigid for time since people with ME sometimes take longer to be ready in the morning, and also lack the stamina to finish the day. Diwan was a keen student who wanted to be able to work but sometimes was just too weary so it was thought that he would not abuse the control he had to call the taxi when he felt ready to work and recall it when he was just too weary to continue.

At 16 Diwan was stronger than he had been in the previous years but it had been decided to keep these arrangements going until after GCSEs. He would sit in a room on his own and have 25 per cent extra time which could be used to rest between questions. Without this support Diwan would probably have dropped out of school, as had the other boy. However, there were few days when Diwan did not attend, even though it might be for only part of the day. He also managed to keep up with friendships in a way he could not have had he not had this support.

Asthma

I include a section on asthma because it is so prevalent. I have not mentioned any specific asthmatic students although there are many, with as many needs. However, they have a similar need for recognition of when they need to rest. They also need to know how to manage their medication. For many it is better to use the reliever inhaler before climbing two flights of stairs, rather than arriving out of breath and then spending the first five minutes of the lesson with the inhaler. Secondary students should keep inhalers with them but it is important to make sure that no one is bullying them. Unfortunately there are some mindless students who will stamp on an inhaler without realising how important it is to an asthmatic. There are also others who are eager to sample any medical substance (drug) that they can obtain.

In common with other students with medical conditions, asthmatic students often miss work and are in fear of falling behind their peers and not finishing their course work. Facilities should be available for such students to spend time in the library or some other quiet area to complete work during lunch-times, preferably in the presence of a TA who can support them. The playground at lunch-time is often a problem area for asthmatics whose attacks are exercise- or weather-related.

Parents

There will often be more involvement with the parents of sick children than with those of other students with special needs. Often these parents have had tremendous worries ever since their child was born, or diagnosed at an early age. The parents can also give useful guidance on how to detect when the student is becoming too fatigued. One common feature of sickness is the extent to which it drains the energy of the student. Often recognising this and making arrangements for 'time out' will enable a really sick child to retain the normality of school in his or her life for as long as possible.

The literature list at the end of this chapter provides reading on working with parents and on bereavement.

Conclusion

Closs (2000), in Chapter 8 of her book, makes these suggestions for schools:

- Show awareness and understanding of the child's and family's aspirations, strengths and constraints, and allow some flexibility around school norms.
- Plan monitoring procedures with the school health team and the family.
- Show respect for and willingness to learn from parents' and children's experiences, knowledge and skills, and from relevant reading.
- Put worried or isolated parents in touch with useful organisations.
- Medical concerns should be referred back to the school medical service and not tackled by education professionals
- Schools should support respite care arrangements by liaising with respite carers and re-routing school transport to and from the respite address.
- Share in families happiness as well as their worries.

Some SENCOs may well be familiar with Individual Healthcare Plans (IHPs).

Jackson, in Closs (2000), specifies such a plan.

Individual Healthcare Plan

What should it include?

1 Child's personal details

- School attended
- Contact telephone numbers including GP details

2 Details of the child's condition and individual symptoms. (It is often helpful to include a pertinent reader-friendly article on the condition. The Internet can be helpful with this.)

3 Daily care routines

- Any required medication – routine/emergency
- Timing of medication, e.g. pre-exercise becotide ventolin (inhalers)
- Programmed procedures, e.g. physiotherapy, gastronomy feed

4 Emergencies that may occur

- Action to be taken
- Whom to contact

5 Responsible adult in school/on out-of-school activities. (Should also include the following as relevant to individual children.)

- Request to school to administer medication and/or carry out certain procedure/s
- Record of staff who have volunteered for training and dates of completion of training
- Individual plan for emergency treatment of seizures by administration of rectal medication (Joint Epilepsy Council proforma)
- Ambulance emergency service contact plan (if required)

Sources of information

There are other case studies from the research but for this chapter I have relied heavily on the literature. I therefore suggest a list of books for further reading.

There are also useful web sites on most conditions and syndromes. Although some of the sites used by parents might contain information that is highly individual and not necessarily medically sound, these sites are useful in helping teachers to understand how parents feel and how their child's illness can dominate the life of the family. When teachers adapt their practice and expectations to make school a happy, successful place for a student with medical problems they are helping the whole family to feel valued.

Further reading

Bolton, A. (1997) *Losing the Thread: Pupils' and Parents' Voices about Education for Sick Children.* London: NAESC/PRESENT.

Brown, E. (1999) *Loss, Change and Grief: An Educational Perspective.* London. David Fulton Publishers.

Closs, A. (ed.) (2000) *The Education of Children with Medical Conditions.* London: David Fulton Publishers.

Eiser, C. (1993) *Growing Up with Chronic Disease: The Impact on Children and their Families.* London: Jessica Kingsley Publishers.

Faulkner, A., Peace, G. and O'Keefe, S. (1995) *When a Child has Cancer.* London: Chapman Hall.

Gilbert, P. (1993) *The A–Z Reference Book of Syndromes.* London: Chapman and Hall.

Homan, J. (1997) *Spotlight on Special Educational Needs: Medical Conditions.* Tamworth: NASEN.

Professional Association of Teachers (PAT) (1996) *Fact Sheet: Medicines in Schools.* Derby: PAT.

Steffes, D. (1997a) *When Someone Dies: Help for Young People Coping with Grief.* Richmond: Cruse Bereavement Care.

Steffes, D. (1997b) *When Someone Dies: How Schools Can Help Bereaved Students.* Richmond: Cruse Bereavement Care.

CHAPTER 10

Effective Support and Present Education Policy

The first edition of this book was about the integration of students with special needs into secondary school classrooms. This edition is about inclusion, which is accepted as the norm in schools throughout the borough. In the first edition there was an 'anthropological' chapter about the second adult in the classroom. The presence of two or even three adults in secondary school classrooms is now accepted as normal practice. What has changed, however, is that the support teacher, who was often trained in special educational needs, has largely been replaced by teaching assistants for whom as yet there is no recognised training and no discernible career path.

Value for money?

The original research was a response to the Audit Commission's Report (1992) where the effectiveness of the support that was being put into classrooms was questioned. There was a call for accountability regarding the expenditure of large sums of money on individual children. This remains a constant dilemma. Gross (2000) writes about the 'paper chase' involved in providing accountability by writing countless Individual Education Plans (IEPs), to be reviewed regularly by teachers who are already overstretched. In one school, untrained TAs reviewed these IEPs once a term. In another school, the form tutor reviewed the IEPs. The latter practice clearly recognised that any qualified teacher should be able to review a plan with clearly defined targets. Special needs was not something that had to remain within a special department.

The Code of Practice was in its draft during the writing of the first edition. The revised Code of Practice is now in draft form but those who have documented and researched the last seven years are asking whether emphasis on individual needs is the most effective way to use limited resources. The arbitrary way in which children are statemented in different authorities, and even in different schools within the same authority, means that there are often three or four children in a class with special needs but only one has a statement. Sophie's statement money went towards helping four students who all needed support (see Chapter 2).

Special needs money is used for the process of obtaining a statement, plus a heavy commitment of professional time. The allocation of psychologists' time for some schools is almost entirely taken up with this process and the reviews. However, some of the most effective work reported by the students was carried out before and after school and during lunch-times. In 1993 withdrawal was frowned upon as being against the spirit of integration. By 2000 it was recognised that students who had reached the secondary stage with specific literacy difficulties needed a structured programme that could only be delivered outside the classroom individually or in small groups. The only way this could be achieved in school time was by taking students out of their second modern foreign language lesson. Interestingly no parents objected to this.

Dyson (2001) points out that although one seventh of the annual education budget is used for special educational needs, because each class in each school has a small sum the money is spread too thinly to be effective. If used for an unqualified TA a child might have four or five hours of individual teaching a week, but if a qualified teacher is to provide this extra provision then less than an hour would be the allocation. TAs are often seen as the saviours of a crumbling system. Their presence in the classroom can relieve the teacher of the responsibility of adapting the curriculum to the needs of the student with learning difficulties.

When students were originally integrated from special schools it was, ideally, with the help of experienced special school staff (Bannister *et al.* 1998, Tuttill and Spalding 2000). In the case of those with Emotional and Behavioural Difficulties this is particularly important. However, this requires greater resources than most authorities will allocate. Tuttill and Spalding describe a model where a student might have support from specialised staff for months rather than days during reintegration into mainstream. Now we have to ask if the urgent budgetary considerations of schools jeopardise the educational potential of these students. Is the time coming when inclusion will be considered to be achieved as long as these students are sitting in mainstream classrooms? For Kevin (see Chapter 4) this seemed to be the case, but that was a late reintegration of an already disaffected young man. His social inclusion was achieved by aligning himself to other boys in the class who had a dismissive attitude to the curriculum.

Curriculum

After an international conference on educational inclusion in Manchester in the Spring of 2000, an academic involved in initial teacher training observed:

> It seemed that most of the proceedings were aimed at the notion of 'Inclusion' and only scant attention was being paid to the quality of the education that we wished to make available to more people. There seemed to be an assumption that the education offered to the majority was 'OK', and the task was merely to offer it to more. (Lewis 2000)

He continues to express his concern about a system that sometimes fails to engage those without special needs in education, and points out that there are already a number of organisations that are expressing concern about:

> the assumptions of mass compulsory education and the balance of curriculum on offer. (Lewis op.cit)

That this has been a decade of unprecedented numbers of heads and teachers seeking early retirement or being medically retired because of stress, has pushed schools in some areas to the limits of their capability for catering for normal robust students. Add to this the demoralisation of staff that seems to often follow an OFSTED inspection, and the number of initiatives coming down from on high with which teachers have had to cope, conditions are hardly conducive to making special efforts for pupils who will do little to enhance a school's position in the league tables.

Nevertheless countless teachers in many schools are 'going the extra mile' to help students with learning and behavioural difficulties. Where this happens these students gain despite the system rather than because of it. Gross (2000), in talking about the 'paper chase' of the present SEN system, points out that although there are more children at the end of Key Stage 2 who achieve a Level 4 in their SAT, there is a growing tail of those who do not progress beyond the achievement of a seven-year-old. Lewis (2000) warns that:

> The ideal of Inclusive Education should be used as a Trojan horse to breach the walls of the current system and to expose its weaknesses. If we can build a system that is truly inclusive of all, we will have helped everyone. If we only succeed in shoehorning a few more into the present system, we will have failed even the supposedly lucky ones.

The National Curriculum with its ideal of equal access to all meant that no longer could special schools and 'remedial' units concentrate on English and Maths, denying their students Science and the Humanities. The National Curriculum Orders had access statements which were compiled by groups of special needs specialists and the curriculum was designed to be delivered and tested at different levels. However, this was before the advent of league tables and the desperate race to push up the levels achieved by every child in the school. Schools that could justifiably be proud of the way in which they had included students with a number of special needs became anxious not to be known as schools that were 'good at special needs'.

While all schools have had to pay lip-service to aspirations towards inclusion, the reality has been a huge rise in students being excluded before the end of their statutory school career, or excluding themselves. If the students become disaffected from the curriculum fairly early in their secondary school career they might well go via the Pupil Referral Unit (PRU) to a special school for emotional and behavioural difficulties (EBD). There is a rise in the number of students being diagnosed with Attention Deficit Disorder (AD/HD). These students have always been with us but the pressures of current classrooms do not allow space for students who find it difficult to engage in a curriculum which holds little interest for them. In a culture where only the top three examination grades (A-C) are celebrated, students with learning difficulties must find the final haul in Key Stage 4 less than rewarding.

Dyson (2001) suggests the governments 'notion' of social inclusion

> overlaps and supersedes the notion of special needs … It brings with it a raft of programmes – EAZs [education action zones], Excellence in Cities, Sure Start, Schools Plus, Connexions, the Children's Fund.

Already many young people in Key Stage 4 are no longer in classrooms in mainstream schools but are in FE colleges engaged in vocational courses as part of the Restart Programme. In places where Connexions have pilot projects, they are working to keep disaffected young people in schools by devising individual programmes. There are probably more young people out of mainstream full-time education in Key Stage 4 than there ever were in special schools as they walk away from a curriculum that seems to have little to offer.

Restart

The programmes that succeed in engaging some of the young people who are excluded, formally or otherwise, from mainstream are often based on skills such as communication skills, practical maths and lifeskills programmes designed to help them to make informed choices in their own lives. There is often a vocational option such as carpentry, motor vehicle maintenance, bricklaying or catering. It is a pity that young people have to be excluded in order to be offered this curriculum but perhaps the wind of change is blowing in this direction. For younger students, who do not fit the academic mould of a society that aims to send 50 per cent of its young people to university, the prospect of transferring to such a course could provide motivation during Key Stage 3.

Mentors

It is still too early to assess the effect that learning mentors might have in keeping our most vulnerable students engaged in mainstream school. Mentors come from many walks of life. Some are trained in the professions, others have experience in caring and an increasing number of university students are also training as mentors.

Successful mentoring must be to do with relationships, communication and respect. Youth workers and teachers who teach in small units have always known how different the most challenging students can be when there is time not just to talk to them but to listen constructively. It is good that the government is actually funding an initiative that has been seen to work for others.

In a research project on alternatives to exclusion (Cooper *et al.* 2000) the school with the lowest exclusion had a mentoring system for its Year 11 students. This was before the training of learning mentors from outside. Each teacher in the school mentored three Year 11 students. They had a regular meeting at least once a week but students could approach their mentors at other times for advice and encouragement. This was an undersubscribed school with 15 per cent of its intake comprising students who had been excluded from other schools in the area. All finished Year 11.

Choices?

In theory parents can select a school for their child. In practice this often applies to those who have children whose presence would enhance a school's position in the league tables, and who could be relied on to support the school. This is bad news for those whose children are on the special needs register, unless they have brothers or sisters in the school or the school is undersubscribed. However, an exception to this is made in the case of students who have statements of special educational need. In these cases a parent may choose the school. There are some students with special needs who would do best in a small school, however in any school with Year groups of less than 100 a child with learning difficulties would make a difference of one percentage point to the league tables.

It will be interesting to see what will happen when 50 per cent of schools are specialist schools. Will this mean that the only students with special needs in those schools will be those with a statement of needs? Will it mean that some schools will offer the kind of curriculum that was previously offered by 'secondary modern' schools, where entitlement to the whole curriculum is not available, but there is an opportunity for vocational courses in which many less academic students can succeed?

Inclusion versus expectations

Difficulties with the curriculum and risk of exclusion apply mainly to those with learning, or emotional and behavioural difficulties. Students with learning difficulties complained that the work became more and more difficult as they went up through the school. Their pleasure in learning had been lost in their anxieties over examinations. Many of them were achieving at a very creditable level for their ability but they were unable to take a pride in a level that was clearly lower than that of their peers. Dessent (1987) suggested that it was important that teachers recognised the limitations of some students. The fact that there is a TA in the room does not mean that the student's special needs suddenly disappear. The provision of specialised, targeted teaching for these students is sadly lacking in many classrooms.

Because of raised awareness of specific learning difficulties, dyslexic students were often able to obtain concessions in the examination that would 'level the playing field' for them to some extent. Nevertheless, they still often had to make decisions about dropping some of their subjects in order to achieve good grades in the ones at which they excelled. However, all students with learning difficulties often found life in the classroom challenging and discouraging. This often led to passive disaffection or active disruption. The interface between learning difficulties and behaviour problems has to be recognised.

A different learning style

For this reason students with behavioural and emotional difficulties were the group most likely to need intervention as the academic work became more demanding. I feel there is a strong case for teaching these students in smaller groups either on site or off site before a crisis situation is reached. When they are excluded or drop out during Key Stage 4 they are prone to social exclusion, and resultant involvement with the criminal justice system. By the time many of these young people arrive in the secondary school they are damaged and disaffected. This can be for psychological, social or genetic reasons but their inclusion in the classroom can do them a disservice as much as it can disrupt the class and put additional stress on their teachers.

Those who support students with AD/HD are aware of the different learning style of these young people. Because it has a label and a set of criteria there is a tendency to try to understand and reframe some of the negative behaviours. An American web site for parents of children with AD/HD is entitled 'Born to Explore'. Equally we should be able to recognise the different learning style of all those students who seem to need more adult attention than others and have to learn to trust adults enough to wait for their needs to be satisfied. Some cannot learn until they have learnt to relate. There is a large body of literature about successful learning situations for some of the most difficult students in schools. A recent publication sponsored by Barnados (Cooper 2001) describes much of this innovative provision.

Inclusion

Inclusion is still more difficult for those whose difficulties are more subtle and invisible. Perhaps those students on the autistic spectrum are the most difficult to include in the mainstream classroom. Williams (1999), O'Neill (1999) and Sainsbury (2000) have made us very aware of the different world they inhabit.

Inclusion has been a success for many students who would formerly have been in special schools for most of their school lives. The students with cerebral palsy have all had their difficulties but have agreed that they were rightly placed in mainstream. The situation could be made better for them by adaptation of facilities and an understanding of their physical limitations. However, this is something which can be built upon. Much of the provision that would help physically disabled students would also help schools to cater for the needs of students with medical conditions. The two schools that had acquired expertise in accommodating students with a number of serious medical conditions had a nurse on site and a room where up to three students could rest.

The visually impaired students have coped well, especially where they have been in a school with a specialist teacher. However, I have to question whether a girl is included when she is accompanied everywhere by an adult helper, and spends her lunch-time sitting on a bench outside the medical room. Nevertheless it is her choice and that of her parents to be at a local school. Other students at the school mix during breaks but a TA is always available to make sure that there is no bullying and that dangerous situations are not allowed to arise.

The hearing impaired students were in a unit within a high school. They had come from a primary school unit on the other side of the borough so they had come into a different catchment area. Few of the children with whom they had spent their primary years had come to this high school. In the primary school all children had learnt to use British Sign Language, whereas there were very few students in this school with BSL. There were definite advantages for these students to be in a large, well-resourced secondary school, with specialist rooms and the opportunity to engage in a range of sports. The opportunities and the will for inclusion is certainly there. The specialist teacher and the TA attached to the unit have trained all staff in the use of radio aids and raised awareness about the classroom needs of the students.

Conclusion

This has been a difficult chapter to write. However, it is a reflection on the research described in the rest of the book. It is a story of inclusion within one small borough which in many ways mirrors almost any other area of the country. There is a feeling of standing at the crossroads and wondering which way will be the one to take. Tremendous progress in inclusion has been made despite the difficulties. At times the road to inclusion has seemed like an obstacle course as budgets have been cut, league tables have taken on disproportionate importance and expertise in special needs has been devalued.

Nevertheless, the role of the SENCO has enhanced status, as SENCOs have chosen this as a career path and some were in their third post as SENCO, each move being to a bigger school. Instead of fitting in their special needs role with a major role in a department or faculty, many were managing up to a dozen staff, mostly TAs. Support teachers were used for the special withdrawal packages and sometimes did some of the administrative work.

Because this book is based on research and personal experience, there are a number of special needs that have not been examined. This is because I have not had experience of these students, nor have I been able to find teachers with this experience. The Further reading at the end of each chapter and the Appendix is an attempt to close some of these gaps.

If a totally inclusive society is possible it must arise from all children being together from their earliest years. It must also mean that all children have the opportunity to learn in the style and to the extent that they are able. This might mean that some children have to be taught in different groups at times. From talking to heads and SENCOs it was clear that fitting the needs of the students into the constraints of the annual special needs budget was extremely difficult. No one was dismissive about what was needed. Many were frustrated that they knew there were children whose needs were not being met.

I ended the last edition with the question, 'How will the Code of Practice serve children with Special Educational Needs?'. In writing this book I have, to some extent, answered the question. It is unlikely that so much progress would have been made without the recommended framework of the Code of Practice. In 1994 my last sentence was, 'Perhaps this document will make the dreams of the keenest advocates of integration come true after a decade of struggling to make the ordinary school special.' The dream now is of inclusion, and although that is not yet realised, the 'ordinary' schools I researched had certainly become very special during the intervening time.

Further reading

Cooper, P. (ed.) (1999) *Understanding and Supporting Students with Emotional and Behavioural Difficulties.* London: Jessica Kingsley Publishers.

Thomas, G. and Loxley, A. (2001) *Deconstructing Special Educational and Constructing Inclusion.* Buckingham: Open University Press.

Appendix: Helpful Organisations

Contact details correct at time of publication.

Anaphylaxis Campaign
Schools concerned about children who have severe allergies to some substances might contact this organisation for information.
Anaphylaxis Campaign, PO Box 275, Farnborough, Hampshire,
GU14 6XS.
Telephone 01252 542029.
Website: www.anaphylaxis.org.uk

AWCEBD (The Association of Workers with Children with Emotional and Behavioural Difficulties)
This is an organisation which links and caters for professionals who work with children with emotional and behavioural difficulties. Courses and conferences are run in different locations throughout the year.
AWCEBD, Charlton Court, East Sutton, Maidstone ME17 3DQ.
Telephone 01622 843104.
Website: www.awcebd.co.uk

BDA (the British Dyslexia Association)
The BDA provides advice, training and publications for those concerned with dyslexia. It publishes a yearly handbook with useful addresses and details of resources. There are local groups which hold meetings and courses in different venues throughout the country.
British Dyslexia Association, 98 London Road, Reading RG1 5AU.
Telephone helpline 0118 966 8271.
Website: www.bda-dyslexia.org.uk

Diabetes UK
Care Interventions, 10 Queen Anne Street, London W1M 0BD.
Telephone 020 7323 1531.
Website: www.diabetes.org.uk

British Epilepsy Association
New Anstey House, Gate Way Drive, Yeadon, Leeds LS19 7XY.
Telephone 0113 210 8800, Helpline 0800 800 5050.

Cystic Fibrosis Trust
11 London Road, Bromley, Kent BR1 1BY.
Telephone 020 8464 7211.
Website: www.cftrust.org.uk

NASEN (National Association of Special Educational Needs)
This organisation caters for professionals working with children and young people with special educational needs. Courses and conferences are held locally and nationally. There are also regular publications on a number of special needs issues.
NASEN, NASEN House, 4/5 Amber Business Village, Amber Close, Armington, Tamworth B77 4RP.
Telephone 01827 311500, Freephone 0800 18 2998.
Email: welcome@nasen.org.uk, web site: http://www.nasen.org.uk

National Deaf Children's Society
The Society offers advice to parents and professionals concerned with children and young people with hearing impairment.
National Deaf Children's Society, 15 Dufferin Street, London EC1Y 8UR.
Telephone 020 7490 8656, Helpline 020 7250 0123.
Website: www.ndcs.org.uk

RNIB (Royal National Institute for the Blind)
The RNIB provides advice for families and professionals concerned with the welfare and education of visually impaired children and young people.
RNIB, 105 Judd Street, London WC1H 9NE.
Telelphone 020 7388 1266.
Website: www.rnib.org.uk

The Down's Syndrome Association
155 Mitcham Road, London SW17 9PG.
Telephone 020 8682 4001.
Website: www.dsa-uk.com

The Hornsby International Dyslexic Centre
Wye Street, London SW11 2HB.
Telephone 020 7223 1144.
Website: www.hornsby.co.uk

Thinking Skills
For those interested in thinking skills, Professor Robert Fisher at Brunel University runs a very comprehensive web site: www.teachingthinking.net.

Tourette Syndrome (UK) Association
P.O. Box 26149, Dunfermline, KY12 9WT.
National helpline 0845 4581 252.
Website: www.tsa.org.uk

VIVID books
For those who use coloured overlays to make it easier to read print, this firm will print out texts on different coloured paper, and with different spacing, as specified.
Website: www.zippedbooks.co.uk/vivid

Young Minds
This organisation was formed by professionals as a reaction to the closure of many adolescent mental health facilities in the early 1990s. It runs courses and conferences concerning child and adolescent mental health. Representatives are often asked for their views by the media when adolescent matters are at the forefront of the news.
Young Minds, 102–108 Clerkenwell Road, London EC1M 5SA.
Telephone 020 7336 8445.
Website: www.youngminds.org.uk/

References

Alsop, P. and McCaffrey, T. (eds) (1993) *How to Cope with Childhood Stress: Practical Guide for Teachers*. Harlow: Longman.

Arter, C. *et al.* (1999) *Children with Visual Impairment in Mainstream Settings*. London: David Fulton Publishers.

Audit Commission/HMI (1992) *Getting in on the Act: provision for pupils with special educational needs: the national picture*. London: DfE, HMSO.

Balshaw, M. H. (1999) *Help in the Classroom*, 2nd edn. London: David Fulton Publishers.

Bannister, C. *et al.* (1998) 'Changing from a special school to an Inclusion Service', *The British Journal of Special Education*. 25(2).

Bell, P. and Best, R. (1986) *Supportive Education*. Oxford: Blackwell Education.

Bennathan, M. and Boxall, M. (2000) *Effective Intervention in Primary Schools: Nurture Group*, 2nd edn. London: David Fulton Publishers.

Best, R. (1991) 'Support teaching in a comprehensive school: some reflections on recent experience', *Support for Learning* 16(1).

Beynon, J. (1985) *Initial Encounters in Secondary School, Sussing, Typing and Coping*. London: Falmer Press.

Bibby, G. (1990) 'An evaluation of in-class support in a secondary school', *Support for Learning* 5(1).

Blagg, N., Ballinger, M. and Gardner, R. (1988) *Somerset Thinking Skills Course*. Oxford: Basil Blackwell.

Bolton, A. (1997) *Losing the Thread: Pupils' and Parents' Voices about Education for Sick Children*. London: NAESC/PRESENT.

Boxer, R. and Halpin, D. (1989) 'Planning for support in teaching', in Evans, R. (ed.) *Special Educational Needs: Policy into Practice*. Oxford: Blackwell Education.

Brown, E. (1999) *Loss, Change and Grief: an Educational Perspective*. London: David Fulton Publishers.

Canfield, H. and Wells, J. D. (1976) *100 Ways of Enhancing Self-Esteem in the Classroom*. London and New York: Prentice-Hall.

Cardinale, D. N., Griffin, J. R. and Christenson, G. N. (1993) 'Do tinted lenses really help students with reading disabilities?' *Intervention in School and Clinic* 24(5).

Chapman, E. K. and Stone, J. M. (1988) *The Visually Handicapped Child in the Classroom.* London: Cassell Educational.

Charleton, T. and Hunt, J. (1993) 'Towards pupils' self-image enhancement: the EASI teaching programme', *Support for Learning* 8(3).

Closs, A. (ed.) (2000) *The Education of Children with Medical Conditions.* London: David Fulton Publishers.

Connelly, M. and Friel, M. (1993) 'Miss, are you a real teacher?', *Special!* (the bulletin of NASEN), February.

Cooper, P. (ed.) (1999) *Understanding and Supporting Children with Emotional and Behavioural Difficulties.* London: Jessica Kingsley Publishers.

Cooper, P. and Ideus, K. (1996) *AD/HD in the Classroom.* London: David Fulton Publishers.

Cooper, P. and O'Reagan, F. J. (2001) *Educating Children with AD/HD: A Teachers' Manual.* London: Routledge Falmer.

Cooper, P. (2001) *We Can Work It Out: What works in educating pupils with social, emotional and behavioural difficulties outside mainstream classrooms?* Ilford: Barnado's.

Cooper, P. and Ideus, K. (1996) *AD/HD: A Practical Guide for Teachers.* London: David Fulton Publishers.

Cooper, P. *et al.* (2000) *Positive Alternatives to Exclusion.* London: Routledge Falmer.

Cornwall, J. (1995) *Choice, Opportunity and Learning: Educating Children and Young People who are Physically Disabled.* London: David Fulton Publishers.

Cornwall, J. (1999) *IEP – Physical Disabilities and Medical Conditions.* London: David Fulton Publishers.

Cowne, E. (2001) *The SENCO Handbook: Working Within a Whole-School Approach,* 2nd edn. London: David Fulton Publishers.

Cowne, E. and Norwich, B. (1987) *Lessons in Partnership: an Inset Course 'Meeting Special Educational Needs in Ordinary Schools'.* London: Institute of Education.

Department for Education (DfE) (1989) *Discipline in Schools: Report of the Committee of Inquiry (The Elton Report).* London: HMSO.

Department for Education (DfE) (1994) *Code of Practice on the Identification and Assessment of Special Educational Needs.* London: HMSO.

Department of Education and Science (DES) (1978) *Special Educational Needs (The Warnock Report)* London: HMSO.

Dessent, T. (1987) *Making the Ordinary School Special.* London: Falmer Press.

Dew-Hughes, D., Brayton, H. and Blandford, S. (1998) 'A survey of training and professional development for learning support assistants', *Support for Learning* 13(4).

Dodgeson, H. (1988) 'In-class support: threat or challenge?', in Evans, R. (ed.) *Special Educational Needs: Policy into Practice.* Oxford: Blackwell Education.

Dyer, C. (1992) 'Which support? An examination of the term', *Support for Learning* **3**(1).

Dyson, A. (1992) 'Innovatory mainstream practice: what's happening in schools' provision for special educational needs?', *Support for Learning* **7**(2).

Dyson, A. (2001) 'Special needs education as a way to equity: an alternative approach', *Support for Learning* **16**(3).

Dyson, A. and Gaines, C. (eds) (1993) *Rethinking Special Needs in Ordinary Schools.* London: David Fulton Publishers.

Eisner, C. (1993) *Growing Up with Chronic Disease: the Impact on Children and their Families.* London: Jessica Kingsley Publishers.

Farnham-Diggory, S. (1978) *Learning Disabilities.* London: Fontana/Open Books.

Faulkner, A., Peace, G. and O'Keefe, S. (1995) *When a Child has Cancer.* London: Chapman Hall.

Fergusson, N. and Adams, M. (1983) 'Assessing the advantages of team teaching in remedial education: the remedial teachers' role', *Remedial Education* **17**(1).

Feuerstein, R. (1978) *Just a Minute...Let Me Think.* Baltimore: University Park Press.

Feuerstein, R. (1980) *Instrumental Enrichment: an intervention program for recognotive modifiability.* Baltimore: University Park Press.

Fisher, R. (1995) *Teaching Children to Think.* Hemel Hempstead: Simon & Schuster.

Gaines, C. (1993) 'Behaviour support goes commercial', *Special!* (the bulletin of NASEN), June.

Gilbert, P. (1993) *The A-Z Reference Book of Syndromes.* London: Chapman Hall.

Goldstein, S. and Goldstein M. (1990) *Managing Attention Disorders in Children: A Guide for Practitioners.* New York: John Wiley & Sons Inc.

Gross, J. (2000) 'Paper promises? Making the code work for you', *Support for Learning* **15**(4).

Halliwell, E. M. and Ratey, J. J. (1995) *Driven to Distraction: Recognising and Coping with Attention Deficit Disorder.* London and New York: Simon & Schuster.

Hanko, G. (1985) *Supporting Special Needs in Ordinary Classrooms.* Oxford: Blackwell Education.

Hanko, G. (1999) *Increasing Competencies through Collaboration.* London: David Fulton Publishers.

Hart, S. (1986) 'Evaluating support teaching', Booth *et al.* (eds) *Curriculum for Diversity in Education.* Milton Keynes: Open University Press.

Haskell, S. H. and Barrett, E. K. (1989) *The Education of Children with Motor and Neurologic Disabilities*, 2nd edn. London: Fetter Hall.

Homan, J. (1997) *Spotlight on Special Educational Needs: Medical Conditions.* Tamworth: NASEN.

Irlen, H. (1991) *Reading by the Colours: Overcoming Dyslexia and other Reading Disabilities through the Irlen Method.* New York: Avery Publishing Group.

James, H. (1890) *Principles of Psychology.* London: Macmillan.

Jarwood, L. (1999) 'Using special needs assistants effectively', *British Journal of Special Education* **26**(3).

Lewis, J. (2000) '*Let's remember the "education" in inclusive education*', British Journal of Special Education.

Lipman, M. (1991) *Thinking in Education.* Cambridge: Cambridge University Press.

Lorenz, S. (1998) *Children with Down's Syndrome: A Guide for Teachers and Learning Support Assistants in Mainstream Primary and Secondary Classrooms.* London: David Fulton Publishers.

Lovey, J. (1993) 'Defining effective statement support', unpublished MA dissertation, Roehampton Institute (University of Surrey).

Lovey, J. (1995) *Supporting Special Educational Needs in Secondary School Classrooms.* London: David Fulton Publishers.

Maltby, M. T. and Knight, P. (2000) *Audiology: an Introduction for Teachers and other Professionals.* London: David Fulton Publishers.

Margerison, A. (1997) 'Class teachers and the role of classroom assistants in the delivery of special educational needs', *Support for Learning* 11(4).

Mason, M. (1992) 'The integration alliance, background and manifesto'. in Booth *et al.* (eds) *Policies for Diversity in Education.* Milton Keynes: Open University Press.

Montgomery, D. (1989) *Managing Behaviour Problems.* Sevenoaks: Hodder and Stoughton.

Montgomery, D. (1998) *Reversing Lower Attainment: Developmental Curriculum Strategies for Overcoming Disaffection and Underachievement.* London: David Fulton Publishers.

Morrison, F. J., Giordini, B. and Nagy, J. (1977) 'Reading disability: an information process analysis', *Science* **196** p. 4825.

O'Hanlon, C. (1993) *Special Education Integration in Europe.* London: David Fulton Publishers.

O'Neill, J. (1999) *Through the Eyes of Aliens: A Book about Autistic People.* London: Jessica Kingsley Publishers.

PAT (2001) *PAT Factsheet: Medecines in Schools.* Derby: The Professional Association of Teachers.

Peer, L. and Reid, G. (2001) *Dyslexia – Successful Inclusion in Secondary Schools.* London: David Fulton Publishers.

Ripley, K., Daines, B. and Barratt, J. (1997) *Dyspraxia: A Guide for Teachers and Parents.* London: David Fulton Publishers.

Robertson, J. (1981) *Effective Classroom Control.* London: Hodder and Stoughton.

Rogers, B. (2000) *Behaviour Management: A whole school approach.* London: Chapman Publishers.

Sainsbury, C. (2000) *Martian in the Playground.* Bristol: Lucky Duck Publishing.

Schimberg, E. F. (1995) *Living with Tourette Syndrome.* New York: Fireside Books. Simon & Schuster.

Slade, M. (1990) *One Step at a Time.* Wrexham: Maysdale Books.

Steffes, D. (1997a) *When Someone Dies: Help for Young People Coping with Grief.* Richmond: Cruse Bereavement Care.

Steffes, D. (1997b) *When Someone Dies: How Schools can Help Bereaved Students.* Richmond: Cruse Bereavement Care.

Stirling, E. G. (1985) *Help for the Dyslexic Adolescent.* Llandudno, Gwynedd: St David's College.

Tansley, P. and Panckhurst, J. (1981) *Children with Specific Learning Difficulties.* Windsor: Nelson.

Thomas, G. (1992a) *Effective Classroom Teamwork – support or intrusion?* London: Falmer Press.

Thomas, G. (1992b) 'Evaluating support', *Support for Learning* 5(1).

Thomas, G. and Loxley, A. (2001) *Deconstructing Special Education and Constructing Inclusion.* Buckingham: Open University Press.

Thomas, G., Walker, D. and Webb, J. (1998) *The Making of the Inclusive School.* London: Routledge.

Tuttill, R. and Spalding, B. (2000) 'How effective can integration be for children with emotional and behavioural difficulties?', *Support for Learning* 15(3).

Varma, V. (ed.) (1996) *The Inner Life of Children with Special Educational Needs.* London: Whurr.

Vermeulen, P. (2001) *Autistic Thinking – This is the Title.* London: Jessica Kingsley Publishers.

Watson, L., Gregory, S. and Powers, S. (1999) *Deaf and Hearing Impaired Children in Mainstream Schools.* London: David Fulton Publishers.

Wilkins, A. J. and Sirha, N. (2000) 'A colorizer for use in determining an optimal ophthalmic tint', *Color Research and Application* 26(3).

Wilkins, A. J. *et al.* (2001) 'Coloured overlays and their benefit for reading', *Journal of Research in Reading* 24(1).

Williams, D. (1999) *Like Colour Blind.* London: Jessica Kingsley Publishers.

Index